JOURNEY TO 100

HOW TO RUN YOUR FIRST 100KM ULTRAMARATHON – AND LOVE IT

NICK MUXLOW

A catalogue record for this
book is available from the
National Library of Australia

Printed in Australia by McPhersons Printing Pty Ltd

Cover design by Designerbility

Editing and book production by Grammar Factory

Disclaimer
The material in this publication is of the nature of general comment only, and does not
represent professional advice. It is not intended to provide specific guidance for particular circumstances and it should not be relied on as the basis for any decision to take
action or not take action on any matter which it covers. Readers should obtain professional advice where appropriate, before making any such decision. To the maximum
extent permitted by law, the author and publisher disclaim all responsibility and liability
to any person, arising directly or indirectly from any person taking or not taking action
based on the information in this publication.

*To my parents, for believing in me
and teaching me that if you believe in yourself
you can achieve anything.*

CONTENTS

PART 2 – TRAINING TECHNIQUES

PART 3 – PERFECT PREPARATION

FOREWORD

Nick Muxlow is an accomplished athlete and a master coach. As an athlete he has personally experienced what it takes to excel in endurance sports. He's been through it all – the ups and downs, and the discipline and dedication it takes to perform at a high level. As a coach he has helped many others achieve high goals such as completing a 100km ultramarathon – the focus of this book. As you read *Journey to 100*, think of him as your coach.

I know from having spent time with him that Nick is well versed in the art and science of coaching. In terms of the science, he has a keen understanding of the principles of training as demonstrated by his own achievements and those of his clients. But it's the art of coaching that is the hard part. I can tell you from what I know of Nick and what he has written about here, that he knows how to adapt the training to fit the athlete rather than the other way around. That's the art of coaching.

In *Journey to 100* he will help you develop the discipline and dedication to train that he has come to understand so well as demonstrated by his own accomplishments as a high-performance athlete. He's also an accomplished teacher, so you are in good hands.

Training for an ultra is a tremendous challenge – one that's not to be taken lightly. The workouts can at times be gruelling. You won't always feel like going out for *yet another trail run*. There will be days when you question your ability to keep it going. You're likely to ask: *Why am I doing this? Do I have what it takes? Am I capable of finishing?* The grind of serious training certainly can become a heavy burden and raises all sorts of questions and concerns. Some abandon their goal the first time such queries pop into their heads. But those are quite common for athletes doing long endurance events. Nick and his book, *Journey to 100*, will help you get through those days. He's been there and fully understands that training for an ultra goes beyond the physical. The mental component is every bit as important – perhaps even more so. His approach to getting your head wrapped around the physical training will help with this. The mental side of endurance sport is the real key to success and something you will learn a great deal about on the following pages.

Along that line, Nick and I are big believers in planning when there's a high goal. Nothing instils the mental confidence that you can succeed – regardless of those questions in your head – quite as much as having a plan. Interestingly, it's not so much the plan itself that is crucial; it's the act of planning that produces the confidence. Nick will take you through the planning process so that you have a guide – *and* the will to carry it through to completion on race day.

Then there are the myriad other matters that must be addressed when you have such a high goal: training zones, workout details, nutrition, running technique, race pacing, equipment choices, tapering for the race, race day concerns and much more. *Journey to 100* will also help you address such important details so that you come to race day willing, able and well prepared.

I highly recommend *Journey to 100* for your first ultra – and beyond. And with Nick as your coach, I know you're in good hands.

Joe Friel
Coach, consultant and author of the Training Bible book series.

PREFACE

I would like to share with you my 'why'. Why I coach and why I wrote this book is bigger than a 100km ultramarathon.

While many runners 'think' they can run 100km, they don't actually 'believe' that they can. Thinking that you can do something is all well and good; society is filled with people who 'think' lots of things but rarely take action.

Often when I start working with clients there is a glimmer of belief. This glimmer is just enough for them to take the first pivotal step and enlist the help of a running coach. Sometimes their concern about their goal, their lack of belief and their lack of certainty that they can achieve what they hope to achieve is articulated when we first speak, while at other times it is only hinted at.

As a coach I believe in all my athletes. I often believe in them before they believe in themselves. For me this is a genuine feeling, and I believe that we are all capable of far more than we allow ourselves to believe. I also have the knowledge that my athletes don't yet have, and I'm aware that by outlining a path and taking clients through a process their self-belief builds. I nurture the athlete so that they grow and arrive at the start line full of confidence and certain that they can make the finish. I have seen it before and know that if they bring the right attitude and desire to the task, they too are capable of achieving their personal finish line.

Outlining a path and allowing someone to shift through that process from 'thinking' about running a 100km ultra, to the beginnings of believing that they can – the point where they start to take action – is the first monumental tipping point. Previously I have inspired people through speaking with them individually, keynote speaking and being the best runner that I can be. This time I decided to put it all into a book. To inspire many more people than I could ever hope to talk to in a lifetime. But also to unlock the power and self-belief that having a tried and tested path to follow can give you, the runner.

So can anyone run 100km? With the right mindset and appropriate training, absolutely. For someone without any running experience, this would definitely take longer than for someone who already has running experience. But the fact that you even picked up this book tells me that you're already a lot further along than the average person. You likely already have a mountain of running experience that you're sitting on. We just need to insert some ultramarathon running experience and know-how into the mix.

Why I coach and why I wrote this book is bigger than a 100km ultra. More often than not, working towards a 100km ultramarathon goes hand in hand with personal growth. The ultra is simply the catalyst. Sometimes this growth occurs during the training period, and at other times is follows the completion of the race. At first glance this appears counter intuitive. But a journey to the finish line of 100km is more than just a running race. It is an experience that shifts the runner way outside their comfort zone. It demonstrates to the runner that they are capable. They now have an experience to prove that. Soon you will also have that proof and experience. Your 100km ultra and what follows in this book demonstrate what you can achieve if you put small meaningful steps together over a long period of time.

It teaches you dedication, it teaches you commitment, it teaches you to shoot for the stars!

You walk away believing that, 'If I can achieve this, I can achieve anything.'

Ultra running is a metaphor for life. What are you capable of?

So why do I coach and why did I write this book? To inspire, to educate, to help people grow, to allow them to achieve their 100km goal and go on to achieve dreams they never thought possible. That is why I coach, that is the bigger picture of *Journey to 100*.

Nick Muxlow
September 2017

INTRODUCTION

Sarah ploughed along, checking her watch; 79km was the number she saw illuminated. Checkpoint 5 was about 3km ahead; she was deep in her race, but also deep in the hurt locker. It was dark, she was cold, her legs were shaky and the blisters on her feet were really starting to bother her. As the track started to climb she was brought to a walk. She ran the usual checklist over her body. Hydration: nope, that wasn't going too well, she was pretty certain she was dehydrated. Food: she hadn't been feeling good for hours and was struggling to eat. Her stomach felt woeful. She didn't even want to eat the favourite training foods she had taken with her. She simply didn't know what to do. Sarah tried to break back into a run, but simply couldn't muster the energy. She stopped and sat on a rock that was far too well placed and comfortable to be coincidental.

As the emotion of the event swept over her, she started sobbing. The course had eaten her up and spat her out, just like the fly you sometimes inhale accidentally when you're running. 'Damn, this really isn't going well,' Sarah thought. 'How can others be hoping to set personal best times? All I wanted to do was finish and I'm struggling to achieve that.' She thought back to the start line and asked herself, 'Why am I doing this? To prove to myself I can and to show my kids that if they set their mind to a challenge, they can achieve it.' With that gumption, Sarah stood up and started walking again.

She could see the flicker of light up the trail coming from Checkpoint 5. She continued to walk, simply unable to run any more. When the volunteers saw her coming in on shaky legs, they offered her a chair that she gratefully took. Sitting down, Sarah couldn't fight the fatigue and she started to shake, her eyes closed. The next voice she heard was a man's: 'Sarah, Sarah, I'm Dr McCartney. Sarah, I'm sorry, but I am not going to be able to let you go on.' Too exhausted to argue, Sarah knew that she wouldn't make the final 18km to the finish. The next thing she knew, she was on a camp stretcher in the makeshift hospital and a warm blanket was being wrapped around her. Dr McCartney mumbled about needing to put an IV drip in her arm. Lying there, the situation started to sink in. She had failed; she now had a DNF (did not finish) against her name.

Sarah was devastated. Everything she had invested in that race had been wasted. Time, emotion, effort, money. And not just what she invested on race day, but also in the weeks and months leading in. All the time spent preparing in the final week before the race, as well as the countless time spent in training runs. The emotion of the event, and the emotional roller coaster she had put her family through as they supported her dream. The effort of organising the trip, and getting up early all those mornings to run before work. The money spent on the entry fee, the accommodation, the travel. The money spent on shoes, nutrition, running clothes and all the mandatory gear. And she was going to have to come back in twelve months to do it all again. Because she couldn't even say she had finished a 100km ultra.

◦◦ ◦◦ ◦◦ ◦◦

So what went wrong for Sarah? For most ultramarathoners it's normally not one big thing that goes wrong. Like a house of cards, the whole structure can come crashing down if just one element is slightly off and the runner doesn't have the know-how to tackle that challenge. The race can gradually wear you down, kilometre by kilometre. You can be left with a distance to the finish that would normally seem like an easy training run, but becomes an insurmountable hurdle, leaving you to withdraw from the race or, even more humiliating, be pulled out like Sarah – so close and yet so far from the finish and your dream.

I'm sure you would like your story to be different. A story where you know how to tackle the challenges, where you have confidence at the start line, where you're prepared. A race where you get to experience the bliss of the final 100m to the finish line, and create memories you never forget for all the *right* reasons.

After competing and coaching athletes for over twelve years, it has become apparent to me that without guidance, ultra runners are going to make predictable mistakes. To prevent those mistakes, they need access to critical information as they proceed on their personal journey. While everyone's journey is different, the key lessons that athletes need to move forward in their running journey are inherently similar.

These are the same lessons that I personally had to learn as a young athlete when I entered the world of endurance events. I sought out mentors, clubs, coaches and groups to find this knowledge. At the time I was blissfully unaware of these lessons I needed to learn and the order in which they would play out. It is only through hindsight, experience and coaching that I was able to recognise the consistencies in what, at first sight, appeared to be a sporadic and disorganised progression.

Wouldn't it be great if the essential lessons, knowledge and understanding were laid out in one place to enable you to make not just fast, but rapid progress on reaching your personal ultra goal? A book that set these lessons out in order, catapulting you from one valuable lesson to the next, and collectively giving you the fundamentals and experience required to become a successful ultra runner.

This is where *Journey to 100* steps in. I'm going to take you on a journey, a journey to the finish line of your first 100km ultramarathon. That journey starts today. We are going to start from where your current knowledge and skill set is at, and build on that to deliver you an incredible ultra runner education that will give you tremendous confidence. Confidence that you're doing the right training, confidence that you're prepared for the challenges ahead, and confidence that you will make it to the finish and be able to share the amazing story of your first 100km ultramarathon.

A good plan ensures the fundamentals are in place early. This allows you to enjoy your running. You finish races, you go on and set PBs[1], and you're motivated because the challenges you face are part of racing and you have a skill set that allows you to work through them. Sure it's not always easy, and you don't always get it right. After all, this isn't your local 5km fun run, this is 100km on undulating off-road terrain, and you didn't sign up because it was going to be easy. You signed up for a challenge, to push your comfort zones to find out what you are truly capable of.

---

1   Personal Bests, also known as Personal Records

WHY LISTEN TO ME?

As well as over twelve years competing in and coaching endurance sports, I also have a degree in Human Movement and Education. That means I understand sports, especially ultra running, and I understand the education and learning process. This is different from many other coaches, who don't come from a background of education. For me, a large part of coaching is educating the athlete. I understand that learning comes through doing, through guidance, through making mistakes.

But I'm not just a coach; I'm also a competitor. It all started long ago when I had a boyhood dream of completing the Hawaii Ironman. It's a dream I achieved, but the fascination and allure of ironman racing continued to grip me and led me to complete seven ironman races with a PB of 9.10. My start in ironman racing set me up well to expand into ultra running. Highlights of my running career include winning my State Trail Championships and State Ultra Marathon Championships, as well as finishing Ultra Trail Australia (100km) in under 11.5 hours on my first attempt. But the race that had the most profound effect on me would be my first ultramarathon – Yurrebilla. I placed second, beaten in this race by Stu Gibson, but I didn't know when I crossed the finish line that I had placed second to such a formidable competitor. Afterwards I found out that Stu had previously won The North Face 100 (now Ultra Trail Australia) and competed at the Commonwealth Games. This was my first ultra race, and my sum total of marathons and trail races completed at that stage was zero. So did I fluke it? Nope, not a chance! Did I work hard for it? Damn straight I did. At that stage I had completed three ironman races and was used to running on tired legs, which helped, and the knowledge and skill set I had developed was well suited to ultra running. So while people were surprised – I may have even surprised myself a little – it was no fluke. I was in my element! But little did I know that that day would be instrumental in shaping my future.

WHO ARE YOU AND WHOM IS THIS BOOK FOR?

We know that you want to run your first 100km, and perhaps you have previously tried to run 100km without success. You might have had a DNF or DNS (did not start). Maybe you didn't have a great first experience, but are now more open to learning and looking for information about how to run 100km with confidence. To sum up, this book is for you if:

- You're an experienced runner, having completed many marathons, trail runs and even shorter distance ultra events, such as a 50km ultramarathon. (If you haven't completed many events, don't worry; you will just receive a super fast-tracked ultra education!)

- You have not completed a 50km ultramarathon, but wish to as part of your build up towards your 100km ultra.

- You want to increase the distance that you can run.

- You want to get out of your comfort zone. Awesome! This is a big step and you're now looking for some guidance.

- You can see there is so much information out there, but are not sure what applies to you as an ultra runner.

- Your sights are set on completing 100km, but you have ultra running goals beyond just one 100km event. This is a lifestyle choice you love.

This book is *not* for someone who wants to run their fastest 100km – that is the next step. The first step is having a great race, learning, experiencing 100km and growing. From here you can continue to grow and set your sights on your fastest 100km or other ultra running goals.

SO WHERE SHOULD YOU START?

Planning is not sexy, in fact for many it's not even fun when all you want to do is run! But a 100km ultra is not a leisurely 42.2km on the road, a two-hour frolic in the puddles, or even a 50km ultramarathon. This is 100km – triple figures – out on the trails. The difference between 42.2km on the road and a 50km off-road event on undulating terrain is huge. From here the jump from 50km to 100k is exponential, as you are effectively starting the race again without recovery!

I'm from the land Down Under, where our biggest 100km race is Ultra Trail Australia. It offers both a 50km and 100km event. The DNF rates between the two are extraordinary. In 2016 the DNF rate for the 50km ultra was just over 6%.[2] Not too bad. But when we jump up to the 100km event run, which is run on the same day and therefore under the same conditions, the DNF rate jumps up to 21%.[3] That is a

---

2   https://www.ultratrailaustralia.com.au/results/50km/2016
3   https://www.ultratrailaustralia.com.au/results/100km/2016

huge difference, especially when you remember that the 50km covers what is considered the tougher half of the 100km course. Looking at it a little closer, we discover that the DNF rate of the 100km was 20% for the men and 24% for the women. This means that one in five men did not make the finish line and almost one in four women failed to finish!

If you're going to complete a 100km ultramarathon, you need a plan. This plan is about increasing and developing your knowledge, understanding and implementing long-distance training principles, and getting you to that final 100m of bliss before the finish line. This is where you know you are going to finish. Where you soak it all in and everything becomes worth it. Where you cross the finish line and accept the little reward – a buckle or medal – which will always remind you of the journey you just completed.

The benefits you will receive by following my methods are many:

- You will be confident at the start that you will make it to the finish line and have a great race.

- You will have focus and a purpose for each training set you tackle.

- You will give yourself the best chance to finish and avoid the dreaded DNF, or worse, DNS.

- You will develop into a strong ultra runner.

- You will have a specific plan of action.

- Your motivation will skyrocket.

- You will give yourself an ultra runner education, and understand how the many concepts and different elements of ultra running apply to you.

- You will be confident that you are investing your training time well, and giving yourself the best training adaptations.

- You will have more fun on the trails.

- You will achieve your goal and have a catalyst for life outside your running. You'll think, 'If I can achieve this, what else can I achieve in my life?'

WHAT TO EXPECT FROM THIS BOOK

We will start by making sure that you understand fitness, both mental and physical; you will know *why* you have to do what you do in training. From there we will go on to discuss training in more detail, and ensure you know exactly what is required of you when it comes time to hit the trail. We will finish by showing you how this all comes together in the ultra training plan, culminating in your ultra race day. In the appendices, you'll find three super-detailed training programs designed to suit different lifestyles, plus the guide you need for interpreting and adapting them. These plans will be based around a twenty-four week (six month) build into your goal ultra.

Throughout the book you'll find the heading **YOUR JOURNEY** popping up here and there. This is an invitation for you to take action; sometimes you'll do this with a pen or pencil, and at other times you'll need to head out the door and hit the dirt. I can guide you and provide you with the information required to become a successful ultra runner, but you also have to take action to improve your ultra running knowledge and experience. You need to implement the lessons discussed to develop the understanding and, most importantly, the experience necessary for you to become a successful ultra runner.

So, if you're ready, tighten your shoelaces and read on. We're about to head out on a hair-raising, yet enjoyable, downhill run!

PART 1

FITNESS FUNDAMENTALS

At the start of your journey, you're motivated. You head out the door and run to your heart's content. But then you might find that you start to fall behind in your training – when the demands of that thing called life get in the way. And as life continues to pile on, your initial enthusiasm might start to fade, and you begin to wonder how you will ever make it to a finish line that looks so distant.

Or you might have been running consistently, then suddenly, three or four weeks in, bang! That sore knee turns into ITB[4]. You're back further than square one! At this point you would need to commence a rehabilitation program, then a return to running program. That dream of your first 100km ultra is out the window, at least for the time being. If only you had understood your body better and taken the right precautions to prevent injury, that race date would still be locked in.

Yet another ultra athlete might jump straight ahead to the ultra training plan, start running well and make great progress, but feel their overall fitness simply isn't improving. It turns out that while their running fitness has made steady progress and they're in amazing shape, they haven't understood the ultra nutrition essentials. Imagine how much further their fitness would have improved had they been open to this particular lesson earlier.

This first part of the book is all about getting some basic understanding in place before you start building towards your ultramarathon. This way, you'll avoid a lot of the common mistakes that new ultra runners make.

CHAPTER 1

MENTAL FITNESS

I bet when you saw the title of Part 1 that you thought it was all going to be about your body. And in fact most of it is. But one of the most crucial elements of training for – and running – your first 100km ultramarathon is ensuring that you're mentally fit and that you have the right mindset. The training and planning that you will undertake on your journey to your first ultra will go a long way towards giving you confidence, but there are some other factors at play here. So first and foremost, let's make sure your head is in the right space. This is all about mindset, motivation and making sure you're jumping on this journey for the right reasons.

MINDSET

Mindset is your mind's ability to train and race. The first thing you need to bring to the table is a can-do attitude. In ultra running, this positive mindset includes your attitude towards training *and* racing. Do you have long-term consistency in your training? Do you have the discipline to train? Even when it's wet, cold, humid or hot? Or do you make excuses? Are you mentally tough when it comes to the back end of a training set or race? What's your resilience like when the going gets tough? You certainly didn't get into this because it was going to be easy! Are you able to achieve a state of flow (being fully immersed in the present moment) in training and racing? Can you endure peak sensation (the uncomfortable feeling you get when racing hard)? What is your mindset on the start line? Do you believe in yourself and your abilities?

At a basic level, a positive mindset is necessary from the start. What you may not have previously recognised, however, is that this is likely to be strength of yours. If you were not mentally strong, I doubt that you would even be considering running an ultramarathon. Come race day, a positive attitude, along with a bit of grunt, will ensure you happily sail through your first ultramarathon. Then, as you progress, the more advanced mindset attributes come into play, such as the ability to endure peak sensation and utilise flow.

MOTIVATION

In Australia we have a hot Christmas and New Year; it's a great time to be outside running and being active. But every year my training partners and I witness the same phenomenon. In the first week of January there are people running everywhere because those New Year's resolutions are strong. But by the second week of January numbers are already dwindling, and by the third and fourth week things are back to normal. What happened? What went wrong? All these people with great intentions simply didn't stick to them. All because their 'why' wasn't strong enough!

So now I'd like to ask you a question.

WHY DO YOU WANT TO RUN 100KM?

This is a question you're likely to be asked frequently. Friends, family and work colleagues will all ask this question. Not being among the converted, they may struggle to understand your mindset. Here are some of the answers to the question 'Why run 100km?' that I often hear at The Ultra Journey:

- To get outside my comfort zone.

- To experience something incredible.

- I always push my limits, why would running be any different?

- To undertake a life-changing experience.

- To achieve something I never thought possible.

- For the amazing journey.

- To reach the finish line and get my silver buckle.

- For the lifestyle and the community; because I love running and socialising with friends.

- I love the freedom – it regularly lets me escape the daily grind.

- It's my catalyst for life – if I can do this, I can do anything.

- It adds the structure I need to my life; without running I'm lazy.

- I made a bet or lost a dare, and now I'm following through with the challenge.

One, many or all of these reasons may apply to you. Whatever the reason or reasons, you must ensure that *you* understand *your* reason(s) – why *you* are doing it. This is important because, at some point in your training, you will need to draw on that motivation. It's generally in the middle of training, when the first flush of enthusiasm for your goal has passed, but you're too far from the end to see your goal and the finish line. You're caught in the middle of the journey, and you're tired, fatigued, hungry and grumpy, and wondering if it's really worth it. This is when your 'why' needs to be strong, so that you can draw upon it. You certainly don't want to drop out!

YOUR JOURNEY

Know your why. Why you are choosing to run 100km? What are your big five reasons for doing this? List them. The big five! If you don't have five, that's no problem, but the first one or two have to be really strong reasons for why you are choosing to run 100km. You don't want weak reasons, such as:

- It sounds like a good idea.
- My friend said I should.
- I won a pair of trail running shoes.

You want inspiring reasons. So, using the earlier list as your inspiration, I want you to list your big five:

1.

2.

3.

4.

5.

With your whys now established, what do you do with it? As discussed above, at this stage you're likely to have oodles of motivation. It's down the track that you're going to need to remind yourself of your whys and access the emotional energy they contain. To ensure that your whys form a regular part of your training plan, you need to periodically remind yourself of them. Rather than create arduous and time-sucking tasks, let's find simple ways to do this. My favourite is to write your five whys on a piece of paper and place it under your car's sun shade. This way, when you're driving and stuck in traffic, you can take out your five whys and remind yourself of why you embarked upon this extraordinary experience.

The other tip I have is to put them into your electronic calendar, whether that's on your phone or another device, as an event on the first of each month. This way, they'll pop up as a reminder every four weeks – just about the time that they start to drift from your conscious thought. This will help you to keep you focused on the task at hand.

Okay then, time now for you to hop to it and take a couple of minutes to embed your whys into your long-term running plan. Do it now, and when you receive your monthly reminder, you'll have a pleasant surprise and be glad you took the time to get properly organised.

HABIT

Motivation is important, without a doubt, but there are some tips and tricks that we can all employ to help support that intrinsic desire. The number one lesson that you need to take from this book is that to be a successful ultra runner you must have long-term consistency. If this is not in place, then you simply won't progress beyond 'GO'. To create long-term consistency, an ultra runner must ensure that two important factors are present. The first is that your running must be a priority.

Everyone is busy, but we all get twenty-four hours in a day. A good runner will put their daily run or runs at the top of their to-do list. It will be done before other less meaningful tasks. The cleaning can wait, the washing can wait. They will make sure it happens. They will get up early, they will run after the kids have gone to bed. Rain, hail, shine, typhoon, they will find a way to run. The point here is that running has to become one of the top priorities for your day. When it does, you will feel better for it.

The second important factor is that your running must become a habit. Good ultra runners build positive run habits into their daily life and schedule, and the best way to change a 'bad' habit is it to replace it with another habit – a 'good' habit. In the runner's case, no running is replaced by running. When you start your ultra journey your motivation will be high, which will help you create your new habit. It takes approximately three weeks to build a habit, so if you've made running a priority, it won't be long before it becomes a habit. After the three-week point, running every day becomes much easier. It's your new habit.

With the habit established, you don't have to think about it much, and you can conserve a lot of your mental energy. Things will start to become automatic and you won't have to work so hard to find your motivation, which can start to decline in the middle stages of your journey.

PLEASURE AND PAIN

At this point, it seems fitting to discuss the two critical forces that shape your life: pleasure and pain. Author Anthony Robbins discusses these in depth in his book *Awaken the Giant Within*.[5] These two forces will influence every decision that you make in life, so it's important that you shift your understanding of the power of these two forces from your subconscious to your conscious mind. This is particularly relevant when it comes to running.

You have to learn to attribute great pleasure to running and great pain to not running. And while you can utilise both pleasure and pain to your advantage, I prefer to focus on the pleasurable things in life and draw on these. At any time when you're in the heart of your training program and you're considering wagging your planned set, you need to consciously think about the decision you're making. Why is it that you want to skip a set? For example, are you attributing greater pleasure to having coffee with friends than completing your run? This will lead you to think your run can wait, but you're likely to find it doesn't get done. You may need to shift a waning mindset. In this instance you need to shift your focus from the small, short-term pleasure to the enormous, long-term joy of finishing your ultra. After your ultra is over, then you can have coffee to your heart's content and share your amazing story. And it only takes an instant to change your focus and ensure your running takes top priority.

On the flip side, maybe you're attributing great pain to going out and running in the cold; after all, your bed is nice and warm and cosy,

---

5   Anthony Robbins, Awaken the Giant Within – Take immediate control of your mental, emotional, physical and financial destiny, Free Press, 1992

and another hour of sleep wouldn't go astray. You can change this mindset in an instant by focusing on how great you will feel when you get back and the endorphins that will be running wild around your body.

To help in your quest to maintain your motivation and utilise these two forces, you need to turn the intensity up. You need to intensify the feelings associated with your choices. This is where emotion steps in. These two forces can't simply be given lip service; you have to feel them in the depths of your heart. You have to feel that pain with such emotional intensity that you take action; only action will rectify a potential poor choice. In each of the above examples, and in the constant barrage of choices you face on a daily basis with regard to your training, the thought of running needs to become pure emotional ecstasy.

When you bring the forces of pleasure and pain into your conscious mind and create a high level of emotional intensity around them, you can utilise them to help you stick to your plan and achieve your dream.

EMBRACE CHANGE

Now that we've talked about boosting motivation and confidence, let's consider something else you're likely to be looking for from this ultra experience: to get outside your comfort zone. Outside your comfort zone is where growth occurs. Growing as an ultra runner and utilising the lessons learnt running helps to create positive change through your entire life. You have two options here: you can be a reluctant learner or you can embrace learning. To embrace learning means you embrace positive change. Yes, that's a scary thought for many! So scary that I'm going to say it again: embrace positive change.

To have learnt something means that you have progressed, you have created new neurological pathways – you have changed. You understand new concepts, you understand things at a higher, better or deeper level. Yet people are reluctant to change. Given you have picked this book up and, most importantly, started to read it, I'm going to make an assumption – you're among the minority who like rapid progress and development and you embrace fast change.

Problems will sometimes arise, but only because you have not been exposed to the concepts or knowledge required to continue on your journey – you make decisions based on the best knowledge that you have. Two things need to happen. First, you need to be exposed to new knowledge. That's why you're reading this book, go you! Second, you have to be open to taking this knowledge on board; this is known as a growth mindset. So don't be afraid to grow and change.

Given that you want to get out of your comfort zone, grow and are open to positive change, I want to finish this chapter with a challenge. I want to help you discover some areas of ultra running that you may not be aware of or may not have been exposed to before. To help fast-track this process The Ultra Journey, the business I founded as an ultra runner's community, has developed a quiz that covers the essential requirements to be an ultra runner, all of which, of course, are revealed in this book.

The Ultra Runner Quiz consists of twenty questions that determine the extent to which you are likely to succeed as an ultra runner. This quiz gives you a personal ultra runner score. Along with a score, you're also provided with a personalised Ultra Runner Report that is emailed to you. This personalised report will discuss your strengths and focus areas, as well as give you specific actionable points and training sets that you can utilise immediately to improve your ability as an ultra runner. I are super proud of The Ultra Runner Quiz and the benefits that it provides to you, the ultra runner.

YOUR JOURNEY

To whet your appetite, prime your mind for what is coming and have a bunch of fun, jump online and take The Ultra Runner Quiz now. You'll find it here: quiz.theultrajourney.com

The quiz can be accessed on both mobile devices and desktops, so there's no excuse. It works best and provides the most benefit if you take it before reading on. It's best to get a starting point of where your current knowledge is at before I start your ultra education. You can take the quiz as many times as you like. This allows you to later determine your improvement. You may take the quiz again after finishing the book, or at any stage you wish to see how your ultra running knowledge has progressed. Keep in mind, however, that knowing and understanding is one thing. Implementing the knowledge, lessons and experience into your own ultra running takes continual commitment to your personal ultra running improvement. This is going to require you to run, tackle challenges and improve your ultra running experience bank. As you can appreciate, there is a lot to look forward to in the coming pages.

Knowing your why, making running a habit by ensuring it's a top priority, embracing change and linking strong emotional pleasure to what you're doing will go a long way towards giving you confidence for your ultra journey. It's also important that you know where you're at with your knowledge, and are willing to learn and fill in any blanks you have. But probably the most important boost to your confidence – your positive mindset – will come through following a structured program. It is through meeting the challenges of a specific ultra program and through tackling the ultra journey that personal growth occurs. The end result is increased belief in yourself and your abilities. You hit that start line with confidence. So read on to learn and grow as an ultra runner.

CHAPTER 2

PHYSICAL FITNESS

We now shift our attention from the psychological to the physiological understanding needed to become a successful ultra runner. I'll warn you – there's a lot of science in this section! But if you want to run 100km you need to understand what's going on in that magnificent machine of yours – your body!

FITT – WHAT IT MEANS

To run an ultramarathon, you need to be fit. Really fit. And the best way to improve your ultra running physiology – your fitness – is to use the principles of progressive overload. Gradually overloading the body causes it to respond to the stress that you place upon it, which in turns causes it to adapt and become stronger. Continual repetition of this process delivers what you see as an improvement in fitness. An improvement in fitness means that you can run between points A and B quicker, or with less perceived effort.

But all this begs the question: what is fitness? You probably know that the word 'fit' was originally an acronym that stood for 'Frequency, Intensity and Time'. These three factors, with the addition of a second 't' that stands for 'type', form the basis of your training program – FITT. Let's now look at each of the letters in the acronym in a little more depth, in particular how each principle relates to ultra running.

FREQUENCY

This is the measure of how frequently you run or train. If you train with greater frequency, this increases the load you're placing on your body. For instance, if you run for forty-five minutes twice a week, and then increase this to three times a week, you will increase the load you place on your body. Your body will respond with an increase in fitness.

INTENSITY

Intensity is the measure of how hard you're running. Going out for an easy run is great and you will certainly make improvements early on by doing this. But if you start to vary the intensity at which you run, you can fast-track these fitness gains. Exactly how hard and how long these intensity efforts last can be based upon a range of factors, including age, training history, injuries and goal race, to name a few. These factors and the way they interact as part of your overall ultra training plan are highly individualised.

The main concept that you need to understand now is that increased intensity places increased demands on your body. Your body responds to the increased load created by an increased intensity with an increase in fitness. For example, if you were to run for one hour and include ten one-minute blocks of hard running, you will get to the end of this run with a higher level of fatigue (in basic terms, you would be more puffed out) than if you had simply run at an easier pace for the entire hour. This is despite each set taking the same time to complete. Hence the intensity that you run at, along with the frequency at which you run, collectively determines the load you are placing upon your body.

TIME

Time is the last element that can affect your overall load. If you run for forty-five minutes, you place a forty-five minute load on your body. If you run at the same pace for sixty minutes, you're placing a greater load on your body. You are asking your body to 'work' for longer – in this case fifteen minutes longer.

As ultra runners we don't often consider how long we run for; the measurement that we prefer to use is kilometres or miles. However, when we look at things from a coaching and training perspective, what you're really looking at is how *long* you ran for – the number of minutes or hours, not kilometres. This is especially important when ultra running. On a flat road or a flat trail run, the distance you cover in, say, one hour, could be vastly different from the distance you cover on a hilly run in the same time frame. Does this mean that your hilly run placed less 'load' on your body? Probably not, and this is because the overall time spent 'working' was likely to be higher in the run that included hills. As trail and ultra running regularly feature hills and sometimes mountains, we need to take this into account. You need to be able to reference the distance run against the time spent running. To give you a concrete example, if you normally cover 10km per hour on the road, then hit the trails and only cover 8km per hour, don't be concerned. You will have still placed a similar load on your body; one hour of exercise is one hour of exercise.

TYPE

Type refers to the type of exercise you're doing. To become a better runner you need to be running, but there is some grey area here.

Other endurance activities, for instance bike riding or kayaking, as well as playing team sports (the more running involved the better) and even swimming can improve your fitness. But the benefit obtained from these is largely dependent on how fit you are. As you increase in running competence and fitness, you will find these other activities benefit your ultra running to a diminishing extent.

Interestingly, while there is a huge and positive transfer between road running and trail and ultra running, they are in fact two different sports and each has some unique requirements. If you're coming from a road running background, allow your body the time needed to adjust to the unique demands of trail running.

ULTRA FITNESS

So, now that we've reviewed exactly what fitness is, let's make sure we understand four areas we need to develop in order to improve your ultra runner body. These are your aerobic capacity, muscular endurance, lactate threshold and economy.

AEROBIC CAPACITY is your body's ability to use oxygen to deliver energy. This is the area that most people start developing first, which is great. It's also one of the most important components required for ultra running and developing it can be very time consuming. However, it is only one part of the complete picture.

MUSCULAR ENDURANCE, sometimes known as strength endurance, is the ability to maintain a high-force output for a long period of time. This is crucial to being a successful ultra runner. The two key parts to this are 'force' and 'time'. The force needed when ultra running is the ability to push down on the ground, which consequently

pushes you forward. This occurs whenever you run. Endurance refers to the ability to do this over a prolonged period. Combining the
two gives us the following: you can push down on the ground for a
long period of time. An understanding of this concept and how to
train it is one of the key parts of becoming a successful ultra runner. Muscular endurance ensures that you have strong legs over the
back part of your race.

LACTATE THRESHOLD is the point at which your muscles start producing lactic acid quicker than it can be removed. The key point you need
to learn here is that if you can increase your lactate threshold, you
can sustain a solid run for longer. You are faster, your fitness has improved. In short, improved lactate threshold equals improved fitness.

This is generally one of the areas where experienced athletes stand to
make the largest fitness gains. Beginner or novice athletes don't need
to focus as much of their training on this area, as generally they still
have plenty of improvement to make in terms of aerobic development. Later in the book we'll discuss how to determine your lactate
threshold and how to improve it.

The last of the physiological elements that you want to improve as
an ultra runner is **ECONOMY**. Economy is how efficiently you're able
to run or, in other words, the amount of energy required that allows
you to run at any given pace. The longer the run or ultra, the more
important economy becomes. This is because, as the distance of the
event increases or, more importantly, as the time taken to complete
the event increases, you are working at lower and lower speeds. This
means you need a good return on the energy invested. Given your
goal of 100km, ideally I want you to be a very economical runner.

Unfortunately, improving running economy is challenging. While economy fits under the physiological elements, the way in which you are most likely to improve your economy is by improving your run technique. We'll look at technique in more detail later, but for now let's explore the two energy systems for the ultra runner.

AEROBIC AND ANAEROBIC ENERGY SYSTEMS FOR THE ULTRA RUNNER

As an ultra athlete your focus is on improving your aerobic threshold and your anaerobic threshold. You need to improve your aerobic threshold so that, at increased running paces, you are still working aerobically instead of tipping over into the anaerobic zone. Improving your anaerobic threshold allows your body to better tolerate or clear lactic acid, which means that you are able to run faster when you enter the anaerobic zone. While you do not race above or near your anaerobic threshold for an ultramarathon, improving it has the net result of helping to drag up your aerobic threshold, which you definitely want to do. Improvement in either of these areas constitutes an improvement in fitness: you are fitter. Consequently, if you improve both of these you will see greater results than if you focused on only improving one. However, while you're improving the body's energy systems, remember that this is separate to run strength, which is discussed in Chapter 7.

At this point you also need to have an understanding of coupling and decoupling.[6] Your heart rate and pace are said to have remained

6   Joe Friel, Total Heart Rate Training – Customise and Maximise Your Workout Using a Heart Rate Monitor, Ulysses Press, 2006

consistent, or 'coupled', if they have not risen or fallen in relation to each other between the start and finish of a steady aerobic run. This is best illustrated through an example. If you go out for a steady aerobic run of, say, two hours in length, at the start of the run your pace would correlate to a particular heart rate. As the run continues, fatigue will start to develop. If, at the end of the run, your heart rate has increased while your pace has stayed the same, your heart rate is said to have 'decoupled' from your pace. What this means is that to achieve the same pace you have to work harder – run with a higher heart rate. Decoupling can also occur if you maintain the same heart rate but your pace drops off.

As an ultra runner, first and foremost you need to build a large enough aerobic engine to power you through the entirety of your race. Developing this aerobic engine is one of the main focuses of the long run discussed later. Once your aerobic engine is well enough developed so that decoupling does not occur, then you are able to move on to developing your anaerobic engine. This does not mean that one is ever completely neglected in the ultra training program – it is simply that these form the different focus points. Your goal is to first develop your aerobic engine so that decoupling does not occur, and then you can look to fully develop your anaerobic engine.

THE UNIQUENESS OF ULTRA RUNNING

Ultra running is complex, with every course being unique. In ultra running you are going to have a range of varying terrain and gradients. Ascents, descents, technical sections and flat sections all offer complexities. Each of these complexities will influence the demands on your body and your heart rate in different ways. Added to this, the way each person responds to these factors is entirely unique, due to each person's strengths and weaknesses when it comes to technique.

While this may initially appear confusing, you have to accept that ultra running is dynamic – that's the nature of what you are tackling. This is especially true if you come from a road running background, which is undertaken in a much more controlled environment. This controlled environment means that average heart rates and paces can also be highly controlled. Ultra running does not provide the same luxuries; this is one of the joys and challenges of the event. You have to learn to go with the ebbs and flows of ultra running. The trick is to aim to smooth things out. Yes, your heart rate will be higher going uphill, but you don't want it to spike. Be aware that if it starts to go too high you will need to back off slightly. Yes, your heart rate will come down on the descent – this is great – and while you may still be running it's a time of recovery. Don't be concerned by this. Your aim is to be consistent and roll with it.

• • • •

Now you have an understanding of exactly what fitness is and the principles of progressive overload that lead to an improvement in fitness. Further, you understand the most important areas of fitness that an ultra athlete needs to develop. You've also had a little bit of a lecture from me about the particular challenges of ultra running. You know that ultra running is a far less controlled sport than road running, and you might have to learn to be more adaptable in your training and roll with the ebbs and flows of ultra running. In the next chapter we'll look in depth at the most important letter in the FITT acronym – intensity. More importantly, we'll learn how to measure it.

CHAPTER 3

THE 'I' IN FITT

Intensity – the 'I' in the word FITT – is probably the most important aspect of fitness. But, frustratingly, it can be the most difficult to understand and measure. In this chapter, we're going to deepen your understanding of the markers that measure intensity, and introduce you to a simple, but effective way of identifying and measuring it.

Intensity is how hard you're exerting yourself when running, specifically the physiological response that your body is undertaking to deliver the required effort. Every athlete, from the fastest to the slowest, has a range of speeds from rest through to max. When training at various speeds and effort levels, the body will respond in different ways and produce key physiological responses. It is important that you understand what these are and when they occur with reference to your personal running.

This is important for ultra runners. You need an awareness of running intensity in order to follow a detailed training plan. Not having this understanding can lead to two problems. The first is under-training, where you're not working hard enough, which means that the time spent training is not as well invested as it could be. The second is training too hard, which also means that your training time is not well invested and, worse still, this can lead to the extreme of over-training. Further, if this understanding is not developed through the training program, come race day you risk going out at an unsustainable pace and, you guessed it, the dreaded DNF. Understanding intensity is essential so that you can create and learn about pacing, then go on to create a pacing plan for your training and racing. We'll learn more about this in Part 2.

KEY TECHNICAL TERMS

To develop our complete understanding of intensity, we need to develop our understanding around the language used in this area: aerobic vs. anaerobic exercise, VO2 Max, heart rate, breathing and rate of perceived exertion (RPE). You need to be familiar with all of these terms so you can use the training zones table introduced later in this chapter, which will be key to your training.

AEROBIC THRESHOLD

This is a key marker in the body at which lactate levels start to rise just above resting levels. When working aerobically your body is primarily using oxygen to burn carbohydrate and fat to deliver energy. We'll understand this more when we look at nutrition later.

ANAEROBIC THRESHOLD

This is the other important marker in the body. It's another term for the lactate threshold introduced in the previous chapter that is a key development area for ultra runners. This is the point at which lactic acid accumulates in the working muscles quicker than it can be cleared away. The best way to understand this comes from a useful analogy provided by Dr Joe Friel, who likens it to pouring water

THE 'I' IN FITT

into a cup with a hole in the bottom. Normally the water just flows straight through. If, however, you increase the amount of water you're pouring into the cup, it gets to a point at which it can't drain out the bottom as fast as you're pouring it in. In other words, it starts to accumulate. This is the equivalent of your lactate threshold.

VO2 MAX

Also know as aerobic capacity (don't get this term confused with aerobic threshold; they are very, very different), VO2 Max is the maximum amount of oxygen an athlete can use from their blood in a minute. However, for this number to be reached the athlete is also well in excess of their anaerobic threshold. This measure used to be considered the holy grail of endurance performance. However, as the understanding around running and endurance sports has increased, this measure has become largely irrelevant. Anaerobic threshold has a much greater effect on determining your performance because a higher anaerobic threshold will help to simultaneously drag up your aerobic threshold. Improving these two key markers, aerobic threshold and anaerobic threshold, will have the greatest effect on your ultra running.

HEART RATE

Heart rate is an important consideration for ultra runners, and the improvement in heart rate monitors means they're popular and a fantastic way to track and help you understand your various intensity levels. However, this type of tracking comes with a very real risk: over-reliance. People become overly concerned with what their heart rate monitor is telling them. They start to micro-manage themselves through technology, and forget to listen to their body and what it's telling them.

The heart rate monitor does provide a great benefit for the ultra runner, however, and we recommend using it in training. The heart rate monitor should be used to help develop an understanding of intensity levels by cross-referencing your heart rate with your rate of perceived exertion, or RPE, which we'll discuss shortly. Once this awareness has been developed, the ultra runner becomes a more proficient runner, as they no longer need the guidance of their watch. Their understanding is now internal. While not needed once this point has been reached, ultra runners should continue to wear their heart rate monitor for the power it provides from a training analysis perspective.

In order to develop this intrinsic understanding, it can be helpful to complete training sets where you cover up your heart rate or change the displays on the watch so that you simply can't look at what your heart rate is doing. Once you've completed your set, you can then review it to see how you went, relative to your training outcomes and focus. If you still can't resist the temptation when running, simply leave the strap (and even watch) at home and just run!

You need to be aware that heart rate is variable, and can be affected by a number of outside factors. Fatigue levels, heat, cold, humidity and hydration – all of these can affect your perceived effort level relative to your heart rate. You need to be aware of the impact that these factors have, especially if you're referencing heart rate to pace, because you could have a great running set but feel that you are unfit, not running well and heading backwards when this couldn't be further from the truth.

BREATHING

Your breathing rate is one of the most underutilised methods for determining intensity. Once you have paid conscious attention to your breathing rate relative to your RPE and heart rate, it can be a very accurate way to help you determine your output. For those of you who are competitive – and chances are that you are – you can even use this as a guide for how your competitors are going!

In a race (or even in training), every time you pass or are passed by another runner, listen to their breathing. You will soon develop an understanding about how hard they're working. This can be very comforting when you get passed during a race; you will often be able to tell if you will be seeing that competitor again later in the race, or if they are indeed a superb ultra runner who is likely to finish in front of you.

RATE OF PERCEIVED EXERTION – RPE

Before power-meters, before heart rate monitors and before GPS devices, there was rate of perceived exertion. RPE is a scale used to determine the effort that you *feel* you are performing at. RPE is based on a scale from 0–20, where 20 is an all-out max effort.

For the ultra runner, having an intrinsic understanding of RPE is incredibly important. A highly developed understanding of this and how it applies to you is the ultimate goal. When ultra running, all the other methods of determining your exertion levels (heart rate, pace, etc.) are simply a guide to help you develop your sense of RPE, or reassure yourself that what you *think* you are doing – how hard or easy you are running – is in fact what you *are* doing. With practice you will become very good at simply knowing your output, and when you do, you will have taken a huge step forward in your ability as an ultra athlete.

The big benefit you will find with using RPE is that it takes into consideration how you are feeling that day. Easy, steady, moderate hard, hard and very hard are all relative to you. With this method, over time, you become aware of your own personal capabilities.

The other benefit is that you automatically take into consideration the time interval you're being asked to complete. For instance: if you were to complete ten minutes of very hard running and one minute of very hard running, you will push yourself very hard for both. Your pace would be different for the two, but you will take the difference in time into account and naturally select what is 'very hard' for you.

YOUR JOURNEY

A great little set to try that will enable you to develop an understanding around your RPE is as follows:

WARM-UP
10 minutes easy
10 minutes steady

MAIN SET
5 minutes steady

4 minutes moderate hard

3 minutes hard

2 minutes very hard

1 minute walk

Repeat the main set three times.

COOL DOWN

10 minutes easy to cool down

The aim of the above set is to ensure that there is an increase in exertion as well as pace over each segment.

MEASURING INTENSITY – TRAINING ZONES

It's now time to introduce you to a table that you will need to look at frequently as you embark upon the training sets discussed later in this book. It's an intensity zones table.

The purpose of this table is to give us a common language to use when discussing your effort levels: how hard, fast or intensely you are running. The table allows us to discuss your effort at different levels (zones) from rest through to max. You may have seen various tables like this, but I recommend that you choose one and stick to it. And given that this whole book is based on this particular table, I'm not really giving you much choice in the matter. J Rest assured, however, that this table has been chosen because it's simple and easy to use for the ultra runner – you.

INTENSITY ZONES TABLE

Zone	Effort	RPE (rate of perceived exertion)	% of LTHR (lactate threshold heart rate)	% of maximum heart rate	Zone information and descriptors
1	Active recovery	10–12 Easy	<84%	<72%	• Recovery • Easy jogging • Start of warm-up pace • Easy jogging pace between intervals
2	Aerobic	12–14 Steady	85–91%	73–79%	• Aerobic training • All-day running pace • Concentration required to maintain effort • Controlled calm efficiency • Breathing more regular than at Zone 1: often 4 steps to inhale and 3 steps to exhale • Fatigue sensation is low; however, after this zone has been held for many hours it can become hard due to the accumulating fatigue • Running pace often used on the 'easy' part of a Fartlek run set

Zone	Effort	RPE (rate of perceived exertion)	% of LTHR (lactate threshold heart rate)	% of maximum heart rate	Zone information and descriptors
3	Tempo	14–16 Moderate hard	92–95%	80–86%	• Deeper breathing than at Zone 2 • Slightly higher sense of leg fatigue than Zone 2 • Comfortably solid • Conversation is start-stop in nature • Close to marathon pace (flat/road)
4	Sub-threshold	16–18 Hard	96–99% (LTHR)	87–92%	• This hurts • Lactate threshold training • Conversation difficult to hold (almost impossible due to depth and frequency of breathing) • Continuous sense of leg fatigue and concentration required to maintain effort • The top marker of this zone is your threshold heart rate (your average heart rate for a 1-hour all-out effort) • Approx. Half marathon to 10km pace (flat/road) depending on runner's pace

Zone	Effort	RPE (rate of perceived exertion)	% of LTHR (lactate threshold heart rate)	% of maximum heart rate	Zone information and descriptors
5a	Above threshold (super threshold)	18 Very hard	100–102%	93–95%	• This really hurts. The effort starts hard and progresses to uncomfortable very quickly. • Conversation not possible • VO2 Max training • 3km–5km pace (flat/road) depending on runner's pace
5b	Aerobic capacity	19	103–106%	96–98%	• Conversation not possible • VO2 Max training
5c	Anaerobic capacity	20	107–110+%	99–100%	• Very short, high-intensity effort • Sprints

Both % of threshold heart rate and maximum heart rate have been provided, as some people have a preference for one over the other. It is my belief that threshold heart rate is a superior form of measurement, as understanding your intensity level in relation to this key marker is more beneficial to the athlete than understanding intensity relative to maximum heart rate. The reason for this is because it is your output at threshold that is a key determining factor of your success compared to what your maximum heart rate is.

*LTHR Zones courtesy of Joe Friel, creator of Training Peaks
https://www.trainingpeaks.com/blog/joe-friel-s-quick-guide-to-setting-zones/

YOUR ZONES

When you look at the table, you'll see that the zones are listed down the left-hand side, and the different ways of identifying them are listed across the top. The table is about keeping things simple, so we use the terms Zone 1, Zone 2, Zone 3, and so on, to represent a particular effort level. This is easier than saying tempo, sub-threshold, etc. Sometimes you may see this simplified to Z2, Z4 or Z1/2.

At this point you have an understanding of RPE and heart rate, and can start to correlate this with the different zones. There are also markers that you may not be able to use because you haven't yet done the required testing. The final column in the table also has a set of descriptors, and if you're not sure where or how to start assigning your zones, this is the column you should look at. As we go on and continue your ultra education, you'll be able to identify the zone you're in according to all the different measurements. In other words, you'll be fluent in the language.

There are two big markers to understand in the table. The first is your lactate threshold heart rate. This is the maximum heart rate you could maintain if you were to sustain an all-out effort for exactly one hour – an excruciating experience. If your heart rate is below this marker you are said to be 'below threshold', and above this point you are said to be 'above threshold'. (You probably don't know your lactate threshold at the moment, but don't worry, we'll look at how to identify that in the next chapter.) You will notice that this threshold is the transition from Zone 4 to Zone 5. This is an important marker, and for ease of understanding, zones above this point are referred to as 5a, 5b and 5c. You are well and truly able to work in these zones, but only for periods of less than an hour. In many a 3km, 5km and even a 10km event, you will operate above your threshold level because you will be running for periods much shorter than one hour.

The second critical marker in the table is your aerobic threshold. This point falls at the top end of Zone 2. For the ultra runner this is even more important than the lactate threshold, because it is possible to operate in Zone 2 for hours and hours. However, as you dip into Zone 3 the fatigue on your body is drastically increased. While Zone 3 feels easy at first, performing in this zone will catch up with you towards the end of an ultra.

Now it's time for a little exercise to start figuring out your zones. For the following set, you can identify your zones based on the descriptors in the final column of the table. It's a start, and as you continue on your journey you'll continue to refine your understanding of your zones.

YOUR JOURNEY

Let's hit the trail so we can better understand how all this works in practice. The following set can be completed on either the road or the trail. It provides a great way to help understand your heart rate and RPE at each zone. Additionally, if completing this on a flat road or similar, you will also develop an understanding of pace at each zone (more about pace later).

WARM-UP
10 minutes Zone 1
10 minutes Zone 2

MAIN SET
12 minutes Zone 2
8 minutes Zone 3
6 minutes Zone 4
3 minutes Zone 5b

Complete the above set once for a shorter run, or twice for a longer run (two repetitions). If completing two sets, look to include a one-minute walk between them.

COOL DOWN
10 minutes Zone 1

After completing this set while allowing yourself to look at your heart rate monitor, try completing it at a later stage *not* looking at your heart rate and going completely on RPE or feel. Then, at the conclusion of the second set, review your data to see how you went, both the first time you completed the set and the second. In subsequent runs you can even get tricky and check your heart rate monitor during the first set, then not look at it during the second repetition – or vice versa. Make sure to review how you went, fancy pants!

A WORD OF CAUTION

It is common for ultra runners to start to over-think things. Understand that you are emotionally attached to your training and your event and to how they both go. It's natural that you want to do well; this is completely normal and absolutely fantastic. However, that desire to do well means that athletes are susceptible to 'pushing things'. If aiming for Zone 2, you might find it becomes Zone 3, or that Zone 4 tips over into Zone 5. You need to be aware, from the outset, that this is not necessarily beneficial. You are an ultra runner, so you need to be spending time running in Zone 2 to improve your aerobic threshold, and in Zone 4 and up to improve your anaerobic threshold. This means that easy needs to be easy and hard needs to be hard, but you don't have to overdo things. Trust that undertaking the right training, in the right zones, will deliver the results you desire. There are no shortcuts to success.

At this point your ultra running education is coming together incredibly well. You understand the key terms of aerobic threshold and anaerobic threshold, and why these are vital to the ultra runner and must not be confused with VO2 Max. You have started to develop your own personal intensity chart. You have a guide to your intensity and can start to develop your understanding about RPE at each level. You understand that RPE is the gold standard that the ultra runner must learn to use because of the unique requirements of ultra running, but you can use heart rate as a guide. In the next chapter, when we start doing fitness tests, you're going to take this further. We'll do a test to determine your lactate threshold, and you will be able to determine your appropriate heart rate zones from your threshold heart rate.

CHAPTER 4

FITNESS TESTING

In the previous chapter we learnt all about how to measure and assess the intensity of your training by using zones, and these lessons will be revisited when we talk later about pacing. Now I want to move on to another topic – fitness testing. Fitness testing is all about a line in the sand. It is saying that at this point in time, this is what you are capable of doing. It also provides a means of measuring your lactate threshold, which will allow you to use the concept of training zones more accurately and with greater sophistication.

Undertaking a fitness test provides a range of benefits. The first is that it allows you to set important training parameters by establishing your threshold heart rate. This can then be used to determine your pace and your heart rate zones. Keep in mind that for the ultra runner these paces are only applicable on flat, consistent terrain, such as the road. When you hit the trail, these paces become obsolete due to all the other factors at play affecting your pace – that is, the rocks, obstacles, hills and so on.

The other reason that a fitness test is beneficial is that you can use the information to determine whether your training is delivering the desired improvements. If your training is not working, then you can look to modify your approach before continuing. Coupled with this, assuming that you continue with your running after completing your first ultra, a fitness test creates a reference point for your training year on year. In other words, it gives you a standard measure.

It can be a good idea to undertake a fitness test a few weeks prior to your ultra race. A danger here is that you might have a poor fitness test, which might crush your confidence. But if you have completed the required training a poor fitness test is highly unlikely, and the benefits that can be drawn from it far outweigh the drawbacks. For example, it can help explain why things went wrong if you have a disaster of a race! What? Surely not! But yes, you could. Despite having all the knowledge and skill, and undertaking all the preparation necessary for a great race, there is still the possibility that you will have a fizzle. Even pros have fizzles! Nutrition, pace, blisters, rolled ankles, faulty gear, food poisoning – the list of potential disasters that can bring you down is long. But by collecting data from a fitness test prior to the event, you are in a position to know how you were tracking and the fitness you had.

Another reason to have a fitness test prior to a race is that the nature of ultra races makes them very difficult to compare. While 100km is a standard measure, just as a marathon is a standard measure, a 100km ultra has much greater variability in terms of the running surface compared to the marathon. Some ultras are flat, others hilly, some technical, some at altitude, some over mountainous passes. This makes it nearly impossible to compare different events, which is why you need the standard nature of a fitness test to properly assess how your fitness compares from one year to another.

TAKING A FITNESS TEST

You can go to a lab to undertake a fitness test and if you're prepared to part with the dough for this, by all means go for it. But experience suggests that ultra athletes are not a huge fan of lab testing. Most prefer the DIY approach and assessing their improvement over time. Given that the following tests are completely free, you can repeat them as often as you like without cost becoming an issue.

There are a number of ways to undertake a DIY fitness test, but we are going to suggest three. The first is one that can be used by all runners, and uses a method popularised by legendary endurance coach Joe Friel (who wrote the Foreword to this book). The second is specific to long-distance runners, such as you, and looks to determine your aerobic running output. The third fitness test is specific to trail and ultra runners, and provides a lot of fun. It is beneficial to test in a number of different ways, as this helps provide motivation for your training and also creates a clearer picture of your fitness over time.

Before you start testing yourself, a word of warning. Don't worry if you don't feel you 'nailed' your fitness test the first time. Understanding how to undertake a fitness test is a learning process in itself. So don't worry; that's part of the journey!

FITNESS TEST 1:
THE 30-MINUTE LACTATE THRESHOLD TEST

The aim of this test is to complete an all-out 30-minute time trial; you are running as hard as you can for the entire 30 minutes of the main set. The test should be conducted on a running track or other suitable running surface that is free of obstructions, interruptions and elevation changes. When you're about to commence the test, start a new file on your watch. When you start running, make sure to hit the start button!

The test is conducted as follows:

WARM-UP

- 10 minutes easy Zone 1 running.

- 10 minutes steady Zone 2 running.

- 6 x 30 second run-throughs (Zone 4) on a 30-second (Zone 2) recovery jog.[7]

- Finish with 4 minutes Zone 2 running.

Take a couple of minutes to compose yourself before starting your 30-minute fitness test.

MAIN SET

- Start your fitness test; take the first few minutes to build into your run.

---

7 This means that you run for 30 seconds at what feels like a Zone 4 pace, followed by 30 seconds at what feels like a Zone 2 pace. Repeat this six times, for a total of six minutes running. Note that heart rate will not fully respond during this time so you will just have to go on RPE.

- Hit the lap key after 10 minutes or program your watch to trigger an automatic lap at this time interval.

- Continue running hard for another 20 minutes. At the end of this time (making a total of 30 minutes running) stop the workout.

COOL DOWN

- Complete a cool down of 10–15 minutes easy Zone 1 running.

ADDITIONAL SET NOTES

This set should be conducted on flat, un-interrupted terrain.

- Make sure you wear your heart rate monitor for the set.

- Ideally use a circular running loop, as this helps negate the effect that a windy day would have on the test.

- Note in your training diary any other adverse weather conditions, in particular, a hot day.

This fitness test allows you to determine your lactate threshold, and improving the distance travelled in the 30 minutes becomes the ultimate goal of the test. Assuming you have given it your all, your average heart rate for the final 20-minute period of the test is your lactate threshold.[8] Knowing this will help you use the intensity zones table in a more sophisticated way. Grab your calculator, turn to the page with the intensity zones table, and work out what your heart rate should be at each zone by calculating the relevant percentage of your lactate threshold heart rate.

8   http://www.trainingbible.com/joesblog/2009/11/quick-guide-to-setting-zones.html

FITNESS TEST 2:
THE 60-MINUTE AEROBIC THRESHOLD TEST

Like the 30-minute test, this is best conducted on flat terrain free of obstacles. The aim of this test is to maintain your heart rate in Zone 3 for a full hour and travel as far as possible. This is not about running harder, but being as efficient as possible in this zone.

Similar to the 30-minute fitness test, the goal of this test is to increase the distance that you run in this 60-minute period; however, in this case you need to aim to do so without increasing your average heart rate. It needs to stay within Zone 3.

The set is conducted as follows:

WARM-UP

- 10 minutes Zone 1
- 5 minutes Zone 2

Take a couple of minutes to compose yourself and grab a drink if needed.

MAIN SET

- 5 minutes to establish a steady Zone 3 heart rate.
  At the end of 5 minutes hit your lap button, and without stopping continue into:

- 60 minutes Zone 3 running (while this may sound easy, it will take focus to achieve).

- At the end of the 60 minutes, hit your lap key. Your fitness test is complete.

COOL DOWN

- 10 minutes easy Zone 1 running.

ADDITIONAL SET NOTES

- In your diary include both the distance covered during your 60-minute test and also your average heart rate for this time.

- This set should be conducted on flat un-interrupted terrain.

- Make sure you wear your heart rate monitor for the set.

- Ideally use a circular running loop for the test as this helps negate the effect that a windy day would have on the results.

- Also note into your training diary if there are any other adverse weather conditions, in particular, a hot day.

Now review your file: record your average heart rate, pace and total distance. It is also interesting to look at your maximum heart rate and see how close this was to your average heart rate. Ideally, for the portion of your fitness test, your average heart rate and maximum heart rate will be very close if not exactly the same. The closer together these two numbers are, the more consistent you were during your test.

FITNESS TEST 3:
THE UPHILL-TRAIL TIME TRIAL

This test is different from the above tests in that it is distance based and your aim is to improve your time. You are aiming to complete your chosen hill or designated portion of the hill as fast as possible.

WARM-UP

- 10 minutes Zone 1 building to Zone 2

- 2 x 3 minutes building over the 3 minutes to Zone 4

- 4 minutes Zone 2 running

Take a few minutes to compose yourself then start your test.

MAIN SET – THE FITNESS TEST

- Hit your lap key and run as fast as possible from your start point to your designated end point.

- Keep in mind that your first attempt should take approximately 35–40 minutes, so that it still takes more than 30 minutes once you have improved.

- Remember to keep things in check for the first 3 minutes of the test and build into it from there.

- Upon reaching the top of your chosen hill or you designated end point, hit your lap key.

After completing the test, take a few minutes to compose yourself before undertaking your cool down.

COOL DOWN

Turn and head back down the hill at an easy Zone 1 pace.

ADDITIONAL SET NOTES

- Aim to find a hill that is run-able and free of any significant downhill sections.

- Make sure you wear your heart rate monitor for the set.

- Note in your training diary any adverse weather conditions, in particular, a hot day.

REPEATING FITNESS TESTS

Down the track, when you repeat the fitness tests as outlined above, you need to follow the same parameters. A common mistake among ultra runners is to aim to increase their maximum heart rate for subsequent fitness tests, and then use this as a guide for their improvement. But this is *not* what your aim is. After establishing your maximum heart rate and anaerobic threshold heart rate, these points will stay relatively consistent. It is the *pace* that you are able to maintain at these points that you are looking to improve.

٭٭ ٭٭ ٭٭ ٭٭

You understand how to undertake an appropriate fitness test for the ultra runner – three in fact – and can determine your anaerobic threshold using the 30-minute fitness test. Along with your understanding of intensity zones, you now have all the knowledge in place to create a pacing plan, which we will discuss in Part 2. Now we're going to move on to another fun fundamental – nutrition and hydration.

CHAPTER 5

FEEDING YOUR FITNESS

Nutrition is often referred to as the hidden discipline; this is because it's often neglected. You can tick every box on your preparation and be exceptionally fit, but if you come unstuck on this one, you will be left walking. This is because you cannot store enough fuel, energy or water on board (within your body) to power you through to the end of your run. You need to consume these while running.

If you don't manage to re-fuel and re-hydrate while running, you risk hitting the wall! Hitting the wall is when you don't have enough fuel – carbohydrate – on board to meet the energy demands of running. This can cause your pace to plummet, bringing you to a walk and feeling that 'I'm simply not fit enough.'

On the other hand, however, you don't want to be eating excessively or eating the incorrect types of foods during your run, as this can lead to gut upset and prevent you from finishing your race. Given that we can't eat too little, we can't eat too much and we have to eat the right types of food, we first need to equip ourselves with some knowledge about what you require.

To understand our nutrition and hydration needs, we first need to understand the following topics: carbohydrate (CHO) and fat as a fuel source, how to read nutrition labels, suitable foods for running, how to plan our nutrition for training, and hydration needs.

Yes, this topic is involved. However, working through the elements systematically enables your knowledge to grow and build as the concepts begin to relate to each other. By the end of this chapter, you will have a sound understanding around your required nutrition and hydration demands as an ultra runner, and how you will go about meeting these needs.

To start, we need to understand the difference between carbohydrate and fat as a fuel source.

CARBOHYDRATE VS. FAT

There is a lot of debate around about carbohydrate compared to fat as a fuel source. To understand what our body requires, we must first understand how it uses each of these substances and its preference for different fuel sources to meet its energy needs in changing conditions.

To the ultra athlete, both carbohydrate and fat metabolism (the body's way of creating energy) are important pathways that deliver the energy needed to run. You need to supply both pathways with their required fuel so that your body can continue to operate and deliver energy to the working muscles.

The next concept that we need to understand is that our bodies prefer one pathway over the other, depending on the circumstances. The key factor here is that as intensity (how hard you're working) increases, your body prefers to utilise CHO as its primary fuel source. Your body is still using fat to create energy, but the amount of energy that you require to run is above what can be supplied solely from fat metabolism. As a result, your body must find a faster way to create energy and so it turns to CHO. At the extreme end of the spectrum, when you're working at intensities in the Zone 5 range, your body is deriving nearly 100% of the required energy from CHO.

We also need to understand that at marathon pace, 50km pace and, for some people, even 100km pace, you only have enough CHO on board to last about 90–120 minutes.[9] Given we can ballpark your 100km ultra running time to 9–14+ hours, you don't have to be a genius to figure out you need to take CHO on board as you run. I will say it again: during your 100km ultra you will need to take on board CHO as you run.[10]

A final concept that we need to understand is that both energy pathways can be trained to improve their efficiency. Just as you can train your muscles to improve your running, you can also train your body to be better at metabolising food to create energy. It must be stressed here, however, that you cannot train your body to the extreme where it can rely only on fat to deliver your energy needs. As intensity increases your body will have a preference for CHO, whether you like it or not. If you run out of CHO your pace will plummet, and you will be forced to walk because your body cannot deliver the energy requirements fast enough from fat to allow you to run. You have hit the wall!

I also want to emphasise here that a lack of adequate nutrition may affect the quality of your training – not just your racing. If you're left walking on your long run due to hitting the wall, the session won't

9   www.sportsdietitians.com.au

10   Apologies – I may get a bit passionate about this topic with all the misinformation flying around!

have the desired training effect. The message here is to practise, re-fine and improve your understanding of nutrition.

A common question asked at this point is, 'Don't I need to consume fat as well?' This is a great question; however, the body has abundant fat stores that it can access, so there's no need to consume fat during your race. It is just that fat, which contains a huge amount of energy, is difficult for the body to metabolise quickly, so CHO should be the focus of your nutrition.

The classic example of not fuelling properly comes from the sport that I learnt endurance training, racing and nutrition principles through – the ironman triathlon. Most people are aware of Julie Moss and her infamous crawl to the finish line of the 1982 Ironman triathlon. After leading the race she collapsed only metres from the finish line, unable to run anymore. While there were a few factors at play here, a large part of this was as a result of inadequate fuelling and inadequate hydration.[11]

UNDERSTANDING CHO OPTIONS

Now that we understand why CHO is so important, we need to un-derstand how to implement this knowledge in your running. The starting point for this understanding is to be able to read food nutri-tion labels. From there we need to understand appropriate training and racing fuel sources.

---

11   http://www.ironman.com/triathlon-news/articles/2003/02/the-most-famous-finish-in-ironman-history-julie-moss-takes-you-through-her-race.aspx#axzz4vLn5Ydi9

To understand the CHO content of foods, you need to look at the label on the back of the packet. We are after high CHO values with low fat and protein values; in other words – we want foods that are high in sugar. Along with this we need to be careful to look at the 'per serving' values and determine how many servings are in the packet or how many servings we are consuming.

A nutrition label may look like this:

NUTRITION LABEL 1

Nutrition information

Servings per package: 1 Serving size 68.37g

	Avg. quantity per serving	Avg. quantity per 100g
Energy	1090kj	1590kj
Protein	0.0g	0.0g
Fat - total	**0.0g**	**0.0g**
-saturated	0.0g	0.0g
Carbohydrate - total (CHO)	**65g**	**94.9g**
-sugars	10g	14.6g
Dietary fibre	0.0g	0.0g
Sodium	500mg	0.73g

NUTRITION LABEL 2

Nutrition information

Servings per package: 1 Serving size 55g

	Avg. quantity per serving	Avg. quantity per 100g
Energy	1170kj	2150kj
Protein	3.6g	6.5g
Fat - total	**14.7g**	**27.2g**
-saturated	9.3g	17.1g
Carbohydrate - total (CHO)	**32.4g**	**59.9g**
-sugars	28.5g	52.8g
Dietary fibre	0.0g	0.0g
Sodium	51mg	92mg

In the first packet we see that the food has a high CHO content, while in the second example we see that there is a high fat content relative to the CHO content. Despite both delivering a significant amount of CHO, in this case the first example would be a better food or fuel choice when running. As a general rule you should aim for the fat content to be less than 10%. In the second packet we can clearly see that it's just over 27g per 100g, meaning it's almost 27% and a less suitable food.

Keep in mind that these are the types of food that we recommend you consume while running, and do not form a part of your everyday balanced diet. Outside of running you should be including quality protein, fats, carbohydrate and fibre in your diet, and eating an abundance of fresh fruit and vegetables. Your daily diet is a whole topic of its own, and well beyond the scope of what we can cover here.[12]

Some of the foods that are best suited to ultra running include:

- White bread sandwiches with honey, jam or, for the Aussies, Vegemite
- Wraps with spreads similar to the above
- Boiled potatoes
- Coke and soft drink (diluted with water)
- Sports drinks that contain a CHO component, but be careful, as some are purely electrolyte and don't contain any CHO. Likewise, diet drinks won't contain any CHO.
- Sports bars
- Gels
- Bananas or any fruit
- Rice crisps
- Baked rice dessert
- Sesame snaps
- Pretzels
- Lollies or candy
- Muesli bars – low-fat versions
- Fruit bread, fruit buns and, around Easter, hot cross buns!

12   If nutrition is a deep concern for you, consider contacting an Accredited Practicing Dietitian (APD) with expertise in nutrition for endurance events. The national sports dietitians association in your country should be able to find suitable APDs with a special interest in endurance events. USA: www.scandpg.org Europe: www.essna.com UK: www.senr.org.uk Canada: www.dietitians.ca Australia: www.sportsdietitians.com.au

TRAINING FOODS VS. RACING FOODS

Many ultra runners like variety in what they're eating. The above list helps with this; however, what we can tolerate in training and racing may be different. When training, due to the shorter duration and low overall stress placed on your body, you can tolerate foods that may not be as well suited to race day. In training you can eat foods that are higher in fibre and may be more difficult to consume. When it comes to race day, however, we want foods that are easy to carry, easy to consume and low in fibre. We want the foods to be low in fibre as this makes them easier for the body to digest, meaning they're less likely to cause gut upset.

Naturally, we do need to train on our 'race foods' to check that we tolerate them and they work for us. After your preferred race foods have been identified, you can leave your racing foods till the final six to eight weeks of your training plan and stick with 'training foods' prior to this time. This helps prevent you from getting bored of the foods you will use on race day. The other benefit is that often these 'training' foods are more economical than a continuous flow of expensive gels, sports bars and sports drinks.

I'm not a fan of gels, to say the least, but love fruit buns, the convenience of muesli bars and the economical choice of lollies. I am fortunate that I have trained and raced on gels and sports drinks, and know what agrees with me and what I can tolerate. As such, I will save these foods for the training period just before race day (six to eight weeks) and race day itself. Conversely, on race day I'm reluctant to use lollies, muesli bars or fruit bread, as they can be challenging to consume and I find them harsh on my stomach under race conditions.

TROUBLESHOOTING

Now that we have some understanding of CHO and food choices, we need to pull all this information together. It's important to practise nutrition in training so that you have the knowledge you need to be flexible with your food choices when racing. In a race you will push yourself harder than in training because the distance or time spent running is longer. This increase in the stress placed on the body can lead to gut upset, even if you haven't experienced this in training. This gut upset can present itself in a number of ways, the most common being:

- A stitch
- Sloshing
- Bloating
- Inability to eat
- Diarrhoea.

We need to plan and aim to prevent the worst of this. Some gastro intestinal (GI) upset is normal, even among those who have exceptional races – come race day everybody is pushing their body beyond what they normally do. Experienced racers understand how to deal with these types of challenges and prevent the worst of them happening so that it doesn't affect their running. Soon you will have this understanding too.

First you need to understand the two common reasons why GI upset occurs in races more than in training. As mentioned, you will push yourself further and possibly harder in a race than you would in training. When running hard your body shunts blood to the working muscles in your legs and to your heart. To aid this it decreases blood supply to the non-vital organs of your stomach and digestive system. The reduced blood flow makes it harder for your body to absorb the digested food. A potential result of this is GI upset, presenting in the various ways outlined above. One way to help relieve this is to slow your pace temporarily to allow your body to 'process' the fuel or food before returning to your previous running pace.

The second common cause of gut upset in a race is consuming CHO at too high a concentration for your stomach. This means your body cannot absorb what you have consumed. The maximum level of CHO concentration that sports drinks should contain is 8%, but ideally they should have a concentration less than this – generally around 6%.[13] Gels have a concentration much higher than this, which is why you always need to drink water when you consume a gel.

If you experience sloshing while running this is often (though not always) a result of having a CHO concentration above 6–8% in your stomach. The solution to this is to have water, slow your pace and allow the feeling to subside and gastric emptying to occur. Then you need to return to consuming your planned nutrition or you will risk hitting the wall later! A common error among new ultra runners is not realising that Coke has a CHO concentration of 10% – well above the 6% your gut can tolerate. When having Coke you need to treat it like a gel and have water with it to help dilute the concentration.

---

13   https://www.sportsdietitians.com.au/wp-content/uploads/2015/04/Sports-Drinks.
pdf Accessed 24 March 2017

HOW MUCH?

Now that you understand the CHO content of foods, the next question to ask is how much CHO should you consume? Again, this is a question that is different for every individual and will require you to practise on the trail in your long runs. There are, however, some guidelines that will help determine what your CHO requirements should be. As a guide, in competition you should aim for 50–90g CHO per hour, while in training you can aim for slightly less than this – 40–75g per hour is recommended.[14]

The next step is to formulate a nutrition plan. This should happen in a basic format for each long run (greater than two hours) you undertake, as this is when you equip yourself with the nutrition knowledge you need to have on race day. This knowledge, along with your plan, allows you to be flexible if needed. When it comes to nutrition, failing to plan is planning to fail.

This is how you do it:

1. Work out the number of hours that you anticipate you will run for.

2. Work out the amount of CHO you would like to consume per hour (50–90g for racing and around 40–75g in 'normal' training, i.e. not when you are practising your race nutrition).

3. Lay out your nutrition for each hour in a separate pile.

4. Over time you will develop an understanding of how much food you need to consume per hour and what the different CHO values of foods are.

---

14   Suzanne Girard Eberle, MS, RDN, CSSD, *Endurance Sports Nutrition – Fuel your body for optimal performance*, 3rd edn, Human Kinetics, 2014

With the above procedure in place, along with practice, refinement and improvement through training, you will hit the start line of your race confident that you will be able to work your way through any nutrition challenges you encounter.

NUTRITION IN TRAINING

When training, you will need to consume some carbohydrate on runs of two hours or longer; under this duration most people can happily finish their run. That said, however, some people might choose to take something light to eat. Beyond two hours, nutrition becomes a necessity. As you have learnt, the intensity at which you are running is going to influence your nutritional needs. Given that training runs are often completed at a lower intensity and for shorter durations than your ultra event, this means that your nutrition requirements are not as pronounced. Given that, in training you're going to shoot for 40–75g of CHO per hour.

This leaves us in a predicament, because you still need to practise your race day nutrition *in training*. Our recommendation is that over the final six to eight weeks of training, when your long runs are significant, you undertake your planned race nutrition for a portion or portions of your long run. For instance, if aiming for 50g per hour in training and 75g per hour when racing, your nutrition plan for a morning run lasting 3.5 hours might look something like this:

0–1 HOUR: no need to consume CHO as you have just had breakfast.
1–2 HOURS: consume foods totalling 50g of CHO.
2–3 HOURS: consume CHO at race quantity on planned race foods – approximately 75g per hour.

3–3.5 HOURS: no requirement for nutrition.

Note that you don't need any nutrition in the last segment. This is because the time taken for digestion and transport from the stomach to muscles is about thirty minutes. This means that CHO consumed within the last half hour will not make it to the working muscles in time to be utilised. This is the reason that, if you do ever hit the wall, you'll have to wait about thirty minutes after consuming food for the effects of feeling sluggish to wear off.

Now let's look at a nutrition plan for a training run lasting five hours:

0–1 HOUR: no need to consume CHO as you have just had breakfast.
1–2 HOURS: consume foods totalling 40g of CHO.
2–5 HOURS: consume CHO at race quantity on planned race foods – approximately 75g per hour. In this case, being a longer run, the athlete is choosing to consume their race CHO content through to the conclusion of the run.

A WORD OF CAUTION

When consuming CHO at rates above 60g per hour, you need to include CHO from different sources, with the additional source generally being fructose. The reason different CHO sources are needed is because of the way in which CHO is transported across the gut – the two different types of sugars need different types of transport mechanisms to make the trip. Your body only has enough transport mechanisms to transport CHO in the form of glucose or maltodextrin (two common CHO sources) across the gut wall at a rate of 60g of CHO per hour. However, the mechanisms responsible for transporting fructose are sitting around twiddling their thumbs, waiting for something do. So, it makes sense to include fructose as well. It's like travelling between two cities. If the train is full, but the bus is already there and is going to be running whether you jump on it or not, you might as well use it. The transporters in the body for fructose are like the bus; they're already present and ready to take more CHO across your gut wall. Given the bus is there, why not use it? This is why you will sometimes hear sports nutrition companies plug a 2:1 ratio; they're referring to the ratio of the glucose/maltodextrin to fructose in the product. But beware of too much of a good thing. The fructose bus has fewer seats than the glucose train. If you try to put too much fructose on the bus it has nowhere to go and is simply left behind. When it comes to your body, fructose being left behind in this manner means just one thing – it has to go out the back. Unfortunately that means diarrhoea! Eek!

HYDRATION – YOUR OIL

Do you remember Julie Moss, and her undignified crawl across the finish line of the 1982 Ironman triathlon that I mentioned earlier? Well, while Julie Moss managed to finish her race, others such as Chris Legh did not. At the 1997 Hawaii Ironman World Championships, Chris collapsed 50m from the finish line while in fifth place. While Chris was undoubtedly running on an empty tank, it was severe dehydration that nearly caused his death and meant part of his large intestine had to be removed.[15] I don't want anything like that happening to you.

15 http://www.active.com/triathlon/articles/chris-legh-s-tips-on-avoiding-an-ironman-bonk, by Ryan Wood. Accessed 26 April 2017

If food is your fuel, then water is the oil. The amount of sweat that you lose when running is often both misunderstood and underestimated. This is because you don't always *see* your sweat; it evaporates too quickly. Have you ever walked into a cool house or shop on a hot day after you've been running, only to find yourself dripping wet? This happens because you're still sweating, but the sweat is no longer evaporating. This gives you an indication of just how much sweat you lose that you are blissfully unaware of.

I once worked with an athlete who entered a hot and humid race in Taiwan. Towards the end of the race he was not running well. It was stifling on the course, with no shade and a belting sun. He was clearly dehydrated, and that in turn affected his nutrition. It was like a one, two, knockout punch. It had gone from a case of aiming for a top time to an exercise in survival. At each aid station, he drenched himself in water to try to get rid of the excess heat. But he couldn't move the heat because he was dehydrated. This was an athlete who was light and normally liked to run in the heat, and he was suffering! He finished a respectable fifth in his age group, crossed the line and slumped on the ground in the foetal position. Despite being an experienced racer, this course had eaten him up and spat him out! Upon finally being asked if he needed to go to the medical tent, he readily agreed. The result: two IV drips before colour was restored to his face.

That athlete was me. Even with all the knowledge and experience that I have, and understanding this subject inside and out, I can still get it wrong. I can still make mistakes. There were a range of factors at play that day that contributed to the situation, but those factors were the same for every racer and I accept the decisions and choices

I made. The point here is that hydration and nutrition are vital and linked. Despite having a great training plan and being super fit, if you stuff up these important factors you stuff up your race; you won't achieve your personal best and you might not even finish the race.

HOW MUCH HYDRATION?

A drop in hydration of as little as 2% is shown to affect performance, and at 5% dehydration becomes dangerous, so you need to know how to prevent its onset. A good starting point is to know your personal sweat rates. When running, a sweat rate can vary up to 2.3 litres per hour under high intensity exercise in extreme conditions. Luckily, when running your ultra, you're not going to be running at this intensity! But we need to be mindful of the fact that we are still working hard and sweating. Most athletes will need about 590ml of fluid per hour, but this will vary according to a range of factors: wind, temperature, humidity and your personal run intensity, to name a few.[16]

Conducting a sweat test will give you a guide to your personal sweat rates. This can also be used to determine the amount of salt that you lose through your sweat. We recommend seeing an accredited practising sports dietitian should you wish to have a sweat test conducted.

You can also weigh yourself to get an indication of your sweat rates. To achieve this, weigh yourself before you start to exercise, then complete your run and weigh yourself again. Make sure you wear the same clothes and be sure to wring them all out, including

16   Suzanne Girard Eberle, MS, RDN, CSSD, *Endurance Sports Nutrition – Fuel your body for optimal performance*, 3rd edn, Human Kinetics, 2014

your socks. You need to do this because this sweat has already left your body, and you need to know how much weight you have lost in terms of sweat. Note if there is any difference between the two weights. You also need to note how much fluid you consumed while you ran. Add the difference between your starting weight and final weight to the amount of fluid you consumed while running, and you have your sweat rate. This rate is only valid for the temperature, humidity and intensity that you were running at on that day, but if you do this test several times and under varying conditions, it gives you a good guide to your anticipated high-end and low-end sweat rate, and therefore how much fluid you need to be consuming when you're exercising at that intensity in those conditions.

This probably leaves you wondering how much you should be drinking. The answer is enough to protect you from dehydration, but not so much that you induce hyponatremia. Say what? Hyponatremia occurs when the sodium levels in the body become unbalanced. Low sodium levels in the blood can be a result of a combination of sweat loss, which decreases the sodium in the body, and over-hydration, which dilutes an already lowered sodium level. People with hypo-natremia generally weigh more at the end of a race than at the start because their body is 'holding on' to the water. In ultra runners this generally occurs because the athlete is too enthusiastic with their re-hydration. They have been told they have to drink water so that they don't become dehydrated, and take things a little too far. This can be exacerbated when the athlete fails to use an electrolyte solution, such as Gatorade or Powerade. The electrolyte component of these drinks means that your body tops up the sodium it has lost through sweat.

So when it comes to hydration for an endurance event, you need to ensure that you are replacing the sodium you're losing, and not re-hydrating just by drinking water. Absolutely you can drink water, but not *only* water. And if in doubt, drink an electrolyte sports drink.

Phew, this sounds complex doesn't it! Let's now tie it all together. You can't drink too little, and you can't drink too much. So what do you do? Aim to replace only the sweat that you're losing and not more, and ensure that some of the fluid replaced contains an electrolyte. If in doubt, go for the electrolyte.[17]

Managing your hydration

Another point that we need to cover relates to nutrition and hydration in hot and cold weather. In order to manage your nutrition and hydration in differing weather conditions, we recommend that you keep your intake of each separate, or at least have a buffer. If you rely on your hydration to get your CHO intake, then you risk hitting the wall down the track. Let me explain…

Let's assume that you enter a race and the weather is forecast to be hot. You know that you need to drink 750ml of fluid an hour, so you tackle this by going with an all-in-one sports drink. The first hour of the race rolls by, and despite a warm forecast maximum the temperature remains cool. It turns out you only needed to drink 400ml and your nutrition plan is now out the window!

We need to build in a buffer and take this into consideration. You need to understand that hydration and nutrition, while linked, are

---

17   https://www.gssiweb.org/en/sports-science-exchange/article/sse-88-hyponatre-mia-in-athletes

separate entities. Any fluid that contains your required CHO needs to be drunk in the period of time allotted for that CHO, or you risk throwing your nutrition out. For example, you might determine that in the first hour you needed to drink 700ml of fluid to obtain your 60g of CHO (your hydration and nutrition are completely linked), but you only drink 350ml of fluid because it was cool. You have met your hydration needs, but not your CHO needs – you're now 30g down on your intended intake and you're only an hour into your race! This is where it's good to have a buffer to prevent this from occurring. Think: nutrition first (this includes fluid containing nutrition) then water or electrolyte to supplement and top off your hydration.

You will notice that we have discussed everything with time as the reference, not distance. It's much better to use time to guide your nutrition, as this is the critical factor. This way, if you're slower or quicker over a given distance, it won't affect your nutrition plan.

The final concept that you need to be aware of is the 'drip-feed' system. Look to maintain a continuous, steady flow of nutrition and hydration. A small, continuous flow is much easier for your body to deal with and results in you feeling better while you run. Avoid getting to the end of an hour or into an aid station and having all your nutrition at once. You don't need to be exact to the gram and millilitre – there is some room for give and take – but at the conclusion of a given hour you will want to have consumed approximately 'xyz' CHO and approximately 'xyz' millilitres of fluid.

YOUR JOURNEY

Now that you have solid nutrition and hydration knowledge, you need to experiment with different strategies in your ultra running.

Depending on the length of your current runs, look to implement the following:

1. Undertake a sweat test or weigh yourself before and after running to establish your high-end and low-end sweat rates.

2. Ensure you are consuming sufficient CHO on runs exceeding two hours.

3. Experiment with different food options to determine suitable training and racing foods, and develop your understanding around the CHO content of different foods.

4. Ensure you map out your planned nutrition for your long run; it is recommended you plan it in one-hour blocks.

5. On your long runs, implement periods when you incorporate your planned race day nutrition to ensure it works for your needs. Modify this as needed in subsequent runs.

6. If you feel you need additional help with this, book in to see an accredited practising sports dietitian with a special interest in endurance events.

Bam! We have just bombarded your brain with a crash course in sports nutrition and hydration. You now have a firm grasp on the role of CHO and fat in metabolism and the body's preference for CHO as the intensity increases. You understand that there is a limited supply of CHO in the body and know the types of foods best suited to replace this. You know how much CHO you need to consume when running, and understand the need for mapping out your nutrition, both in training and when racing. You understand hydration requirements and why it's important not to get dehydrated when racing. Implementing these lessons and concepts will ensure that your training improves. You will feel better before, during and after running, and be able to run strongly for your entire race because your body has the necessary fuel and fluid on board to power you through. You are a nutrition and hydration queen ... or king! If you feel a little overwhelmed at this stage, don't worry – that is quite normal. As you implement your newly acquired knowledge in your training, you will increase your confidence in this area. As Benjamin Franklin said, 'Tell me and I forget, teach me and I may remember, involve me and I learn.'

PART 2

TRAINING TECHNIQUES

Okay, I promise you that all the heavy science stuff is now over. But I'm glad you ploughed your way through everything, because now you have a fantastic understanding of the important fundamentals that will underpin not just your training, but your first 100km ultra. And second, and third…

In this second part of the book you're going to hit the ground running – literally! You'll learn all about the different training sets that will ultimately form the content of the training plans that are discussed in Part 3. Next we'll move on to the specific techniques that you need to undertake the ultimate challenge – running 100km and crossing the finishing line feeling like you're on top of the world. Finally there's a whole chapter devoted to the all-important topic of pacing, and the heavy work we did in Part 1 means you'll be able to understand where this is coming from and how to build it into your training. Right then, let's get to it.

CHAPTER 6

TRAINING SETS

Earlier in the book you developed your understanding around intensity and how to establish your training zones from a fitness test. The next topic that we need to develop is our understanding of the different training sets that can be used to improve your ultra running fitness. You need to understand what the different sets are, the benefits that they provide and how to 'run' the different sets. Your understanding around intensity zones gains greater relevance here, as it provides a common language that allows us to discuss the effort and intensity required in the training sets.

If you choose not to employ the following training sets and ultra training methods, you risk not having developed a strong enough aerobic engine to power you through your full 100km. You also run the risk of not having the leg strength required to finish your 100km running strong! You want to finish strong, right? For this you are going to need an insane aerobic engine and highly developed leg strength to get you up the mountains, down the hills and over the rocky, rutted, sandy and root-covered paths that line your route.

The training sets that you need to understand are:

- Long run
- Interval session
- Fartlek session
- Tempo run

- Recovery run
- Soul run

It is essential that you have a well-balanced ultra running program. This means including the above sessions at strategic times – simply going out for an easy or moderate run each time you train is not the quickest or most time-effective way to improve your fitness. You also need to understand how to complete a thorough warm-up and an appropriate cool down. At the end of this book you'll find the appendices with all this variety packed into three detailed training programs, but for now I want to continue with your education and make sure you know how to nail each of these sets.

THE WARM-UP & COOL DOWN

A warm-up and cool down are an essential part of any training set. A warm-up involves easy running at the start of a set and gradually building your intensity. Part of the warm-up may include segments of harder running interspersed with segments of easier running.

You need to complete a warm-up because it prepares your body and mind for the session ahead. There are many changes that take place during the warm-up, but the most important ones can be summarised as follows:

- Increased blood temperature, allowing oxygen to more easily bind to the red blood cells.
- Improved blood flow to the working muscles and away from non-essential functions.

- Improved elasticity of the muscles, helping to decrease the risk of injury.

At the end of your warm-up, you should have a light sweat and be mentally and physically ready for the session ahead.

There are a number of ways to complete a succinct and effective warm-up. Having three standard options work well, as once they're learnt you don't have to think too much about your warm-up. This allows you to relax and enjoy your running. If running in the morning, all you have to do is simply smell the roses, while running in the afternoon means you can escape the stress of the day.

The main thing with each of the following warm-ups is that you don't want to feel the need to 'push' the pace during this time. Let your running naturally come to you as you warm-up. When it's cold, you will notice that it takes longer for your core temperature to rise and therefore longer for this pace to naturally come to you. No surprises there, right? ☺

Each of the following warm-ups is paired with a specific running set.

WARM-UP 1 – FOR YOUR LONG RUN OR STEADY STATE RUN
10 minutes easy Zone 1 running.
10 minutes building from Zone 1 to Zone 2, allowing you to naturally build to Zone 2 during this time and into your steady state or long run.

WARM-UP 2 – INTERVAL SET WARM-UP
10 minutes easy Zone 1 running, allowing you to naturally build to Zone 2 at the conclusion.

4 x 1-minute strides:

- These are completed on a 1-minute Zone 2 recovery; i.e. you run hard for 1 minute, then run easy for 1 minute, taking 8 minutes total.

- You will likely find that on the first two you reach a Zone 3 level, and on the final two you approach a Zone 4 level.

2 minutes Zone 2 running to finish.

WARM-UP 3 – FARTLEK WARM-UP
10 minutes easy Zone 1 running, allowing yourself to naturally build towards Zone 2 at the conclusion.
2 x 3-mintue builds (building your pace over the three minutes from Zone 2 towards a Zone 4 effort).
4 minutes easy Zone 2 running.

COOL DOWN
It's important that you don't overlook the cool down. You complete a cool down to prevent the blood and associated by-products of exercise from pooling in the legs. Your aim is to gradually return the body to a pre-exercise state. Rather than seeing the cool down as the conclusion of the session, look at it as a means of ensuring you run well in your next session. This little mindset shift makes a big difference with how ultra runners view the cool down.

To prevent confusion, the cool down should be kept super-simple and consistent.

At the end of a long run, a cool down is as easy as completing five minutes Zone 1 running. If the cool down is at the conclusion of a set that included intensity block(s), ten minutes of easy Zone 1 running is recommended.

In addition to these standard cool downs, it's beneficial to walk for three to five minutes. However, time constrains involving kids, work and life sometimes prevent this, so the three to five-minute walk is an optional extra at the conclusion of every set. You get a gold star if you do it, though!

THE LONG RUN

The long run is your most important training session of the week. Not surprisingly it's generally the favourite training session of the ultra runner, which is fantastic. The long run is the set that most closely relates to the demands of the ultra runner. It is, as it sounds, long and steady. This session will:

- Improve your aerobic energy systems and ultra runner body.
- Improve your muscular endurance (running strong).
- Allow you to develop long-distance pace awareness.
- Allow you to practise your race nutrition.
- Help to develop your ultra runner mindset, preparing you for the challenge ahead.
- Give you a chance to practise power walking in race-like conditions.
- Provide an opportunity to focus and improve in additional areas, such as gear use, uphills, downhills or cadence work.
- Gets you used to spending long periods of time running.

The specifics of the long run are determined by how the session is structured and what its objectives are. At the start of a training program, the long run may be as little as 80 minutes, and at the upper end it may be 5+ hours. While the long run will often be a steady Zone 1/2 run, at times efforts at higher zones may be incorporated.

It's recommended that you only increase the distance or duration of any one set by increments of 10%. So while an athlete running 80 minutes can extend this to 88 minutes the following week, the ultra runner can extend a 180-minute run by 18 minutes and complete 198 minutes the following week. While in a strict sense this is okay, you also need to be aware of the running and load that has occurred through the week. How this load progression is implemented will become much clearer when training plans are discussed in Part 3.

INTERVAL SESSION

The interval session is all about hard to very hard running – Zone 4 and above – followed by periods of recovery.

Zone 4 interval running is a staple of the ultra runner, despite Zone 4 being far in excess of the speed maintained on race day. It is at this point that lactate threshold is being taxed, but because the pace maintained is slightly *below* threshold, a larger amount of 'work' can be achieved than when the body is tipped *above* threshold.

Intervals of Zone 5 running are also used, as this type of training creates improvements in the mitochondria make-up of the cells. (The mitochondria are the site of energy production in the body.) In simpler terms, a little bit of high intensity work goes a long way to improving your body's capacity to make energy – that is, it makes you fitter.

It's important to note that high-end Zone 5 training is used sparingly, and it's not the improvement in leg speed that you're after, but the heart rate response. That means that you shouldn't be 'pushing' – you must always be running in control and with good form. Heart rate will naturally respond to hard running.

Ultra runners should normally complete these sessions on hills, which provide added strength endurance and reduce the risk of injury. This is discussed in depth in the next chapter. The time period of these intervals is often longer (10 to 30 minutes) than what a road marathoner would be used to, and as such the pace maintained is lower. This allows the cumulative time spent 'working' to be higher, thus being more closely related to the ultra runner's requirements.

The recovery period of the interval run is essential, as the physical and mental demands of this high intensity running are very challenging, particularly *outside* race conditions. In a traditional interval set the rest period is stationary; however, since training techniques and the understanding of training has improved, it has been found that completing this recovery as a walk into a slow jog is better. This is beneficial because it helps to keep the blood flowing to the legs and the heart rate slightly elevated, which improves the quality of the following interval.

Finally, it's important to note that, no matter your ability, you should build into these sessions. If you have a history of injury or are recovering from an injury, it is recommended that you skip these segments until you can safely complete them.

FARTLEK SESSION

Fartlek means 'speed play' in Swedish, and a fartlek session is when you vary your speed as you run. This could be through a range of speeds or just a few, with segments of hard running followed by segments of easier running.

The key difference between an interval and a fartlek session is the speed at which the 'recovery' portion of the run is completed. In intervals we are moving almost for the sake of moving during the recovery period, because the intense component was, well … intense. But with a fartlek run, the speed held during the recovery period is much quicker, with an active recovery normally in Zone 2 or higher.

Like an interval session, a fartlek session can be completed on the trails or on the road. However, the higher pace of the recovery portion means that the effort portion of a fartlek session must be completed at either a lower intensity or reduced duration, as compared to an interval session.

As a trail and ultra runner you achieve a fartlek run, or something close to it, on almost every long run you do, as hills naturally cause this effect on your running. If you are forced to run on the road through the week, completing fartlek training is a great help, as it mimics the demands of trail running more closely.

A key mistake that newer ultra runners make is that they focus solely on making the distance, and remove interval and fartlek training from their weekly program. As a result their fitness does not improve as quickly as it would if they retained this type of training.

The fartlek and interval sessions are a fantastic way to train. Due to the increased demands placed on your body for short periods, they are more effective at improving your fitness than only going out for an easy or moderate run. Therefore, a session that features changes in intensity becomes your second most important run of the week, with the long run being the most important.

TEMPO SESSION

The tempo session relates to the tempo zone (Zone 3). This is the zone ultra runners love: comfortably solid, controlled, calm efficiency. It's fast so that you feel you're running well, but not so fast that you're uncomfortable, as you might be at a Zone 4 or Zone 5 pace. Due to the lower intensity, large blocks of time can be achieved. This is often the zone you will find yourself in when climbing hills. There are a number of ways in which this session can be structured in your training, allowing the tempo session to occur on the flat or on the trails.

Due to the good feeling associated with working at this pace, it's important to make sure the speed of a long run, or even a recovery run, does not creep above Zone 2 (unless specifically stated). Too much time at a Zone 3 pace can lead to over-training. This means you may be too fatigued to hit higher zones during your interval and fartlek runs as you have wiped yourself out during your long run.

RECOVERY RUN & STEADY STATE RUN

A recovery run and steady state run are very similar in nature to the weekly long run; however, the focus of the session and the accumulative time taken are vastly different. This is why they need to be discussed separately. It's also helpful for these sessions to have a different name – this helps you approach the session with the right mindset and achieve the correct, specific outcomes.

A recovery run is – as it sounds – about helping the legs recover. Depending on how long you have been running, a recovery day may be a day off running, or it may simply be an easy run. The aim of a recovery run is to promote blood flow to the legs and aid in recovery. As such, it is completed at an easy Zone 1 to Zone 2 level and will be quite short. The focus is purely on improved blood flow to the legs to aid in recovery.

The steady state run is more closely related in nature to the long run, but is much shorter. These runs are all about adding additional volume or load to the run program, and are conducted with a focus on Zone 2 running. Depending on your experience as a runner and the number of times you run per week, these sessions may or may not be present, as they're nowhere near as important as the sessions discussed above.

THE SOUL RUN

The soul run is a term used at The Ultra Journey to explain that you're going out for a run purely to enjoy it. With the other sessions, you may be following different times, focus points and training objectives, and it can all become a bit much! You need to make sure you remember why you run and regularly connect with the essence of being an ultra runner and the reasons why you got into running.

There is still a set time for this run, however, because without a time limit some ultra runners would take this as a free ticket to run all day! But time is the only parameter; outside of that it's running for the freedom and enjoyment of running.

You may be wondering at this point exactly what your training schedule is going to look like – how many runs per week, how long your long run will be, how many interval sessions you need and so on. But don't worry, the point of the discussion here is to educate you about how to approach each type of run. Later, in Chapter 14, we'll discuss training plans in more detail, and in the appendices you'll find three fully spec'd training plans revealed in all their glorious detail. (Hmm, do I hear the sound of pages being turned?)

◦◦ ◦◦ ◦◦ ◦◦

You now have a clear understanding of the different running sets that can be used in the ultra runner program: the long run; intensity sets, including interval sets and fartlek runs; and tempo sessions. You have an appreciation of recovery runs, steady state runs and soul runs, and understand the aims and objectives of each. However, to fully come to grips with these sessions, in your body *and* mind, you are going to have to practise them. You won't be an 'expert' at these immediately; you will have to continue to practise and improve, and this may take many runs. But simply by going into a set with a goal and an objective that challenges you, you will be helping to progress your running. There is no need to be overwhelmed; even if you are not yet there with your understanding of these sets, your run fitness and understanding of your personal capabilities will already be improving, and that is fantastic.

The key take-away is that you have to get out there and run; experiment and try different sets, and challenge yourself! It will all start to come together. Whatever happens, remember, 'just keep running!'

CHAPTER 7

ULTRA TECHNIQUES

Beyond the training sets discussed in the previous chapter, you also need to utilise specific long-distance training techniques to ensure that your training program is properly geared towards ultra running and completing your first 100km ultramarathon.

The ultra techniques discussed here are all designed to build your runner strength, both physically and mentally, to ensure you are up for the challenge ahead. While these sessions will ensure that you have an ultra journey body that's ready to run, they're also about developing confidence in your personal running ability; you will *know* that you're capable of both making the distance and running well for the entire duration of the race.

The techniques that you utilise as an ultramarathoner are double run days and their extension, double run weekends. You also need to ensure runner strength is in place. Yes, it's talked about a lot, but your run strength is essential to your success. To this end, you are going to become accustomed to hills. Hills, hills, hills and more hills! You also need to do what you can to improve your cadence. And finally, you need to include race simulation training in the mix.

It's important to incorporate these ultra techniques in your game plan because they're highly specific, but an additional benefit is that they make training more fun. You have variety across your plan, with many different focus points and challenges to engage you and help you progress.

These training sets are hard; they will challenge you, but that is all part of ensuring that you're confident at the start of your race that you will make the finish line. They also help to ensure your fitness improves at a quicker rate, but that's really just a bonus to all the fun you're going to have!

The usual risks apply if you choose not to follow these guidelines – DNFs and a lack of confidence, or indeed *no* confidence, at the start line. Now imagine you're at that start line for a moment – see that competitor standing next to you on the start line? If you follow these guidelines, it's doubtful they will have as much fun as you on race day. You have included these techniques in your training and learnt the valuable lessons that they provide. And on we run!

DOUBLE RUN DAYS & DOUBLE RUN WEEKENDS

Double runs days and their extension, double run weekends, are a great way to increase run volume while lowering the risk of injury that completing a similar run volume in one session carries. A double run day is when two runs are completed on one day: one in the morning and one in the afternoon. A double run weekend is when two longer runs are completed one day after another – one on Saturday and one on Sunday. When structured this way, the cumulative load across both runs and/or days needs to be taken into account.

The key point in this approach is that it allows for a recovery and re-fuelling period between runs. Utilising this strategy often works at the midway point in an ultra runner's training, when they're looking to step up the distance of their long run. They might need this strategy because they're new to ultra running, or maybe they're looking to tackle a longer race – perhaps a 100km. But the approach is valid for every runner, regardless of ability, as volume is relative to the individual. So, what does it look like in practice?

A mid-week double run could involve two shorter runs that collectively give you a significant total volume. And as your program progresses, you will often implement a double long run weekend. This is a fantastic way to prepare your body for the demands of your ultra. In both cases you need to look at the runs as a collective session, and be aware of the cumulative fatigue and effect that they will have on your body. You need to understand this *before* you begin a double session, because you need to allow enough fuel in the tank to be able to complete the second session, whether that takes place in the afternoon or on the following day. This means you need to keep the first session in control, which involves sticking to the training plan and not overdoing things. Don't let the relative ease of a shorter first session trick you into pushing it. Trust me when I tell you that once the second session has been completed, you will be much more fatigued than you might expect. If you fail on this advice, you'll learn through experience on this one. After you have completed a couple of these types of sets, it becomes much easier to hold back on the first session – you know you need to be able to back up and run again later.

CADENCE WORK

Run pace, the speed at which you run, is dictated by two variables: stride length and stride frequency, or cadence. Cadence is the number of times your foot strikes the ground per minute. To increase your pace, you can either increase your stride length or increase your cadence. Similarly, to decrease your pace, you can decrease your stride length or decrease your cadence. 'So what?' I hear you say.

If cadence is a concern, then it's likely to be too low rather than too high. Improving your cadence towards the range of 88+ strides per minute, when running on the flat, should become a goal. This will make running easy, efficient and more enjoyable. To achieve this, you may need to decrease your stride length to be able to increase your cadence. Confused? Yes? Let me explain.

Your muscles work in a similar way to a rubber band. If a rubber band is just sitting there, minding its own business, there is no energy stored in it. However, if you stretch the rubber band, you can fling it across the room using its stored energy. When your cadence hits the 88+ strides per minute range, your run efficiency improves because you are able to store some of the energy you have already generated and use it in your next stride.

This can be demonstrated by performing a jumping exercise. If you're sitting down, jump up and find a wall to stand next to. Now bend down and touch your toes. Pause a moment. From this crouched position, spring up and jump as high as you can. Tap the wall to get an indication of how high you can jump. Now repeat the exercise, but this time in one complete motion. Go from standing to the crouched position then, without stopping, explode up. You should be able to jump much higher the second time. When you don't take that pause, there's still energy stored in your muscles that you then access as you jump up.

This same principle applies to your running. When your cadence approaches 90 strides per minute, you have decreased the pause between strides enough to access the energy you have already generated – free energy. Below this rate, this energy is lost.

YOUR JOURNEY

The best way to work towards this improvement is through small increments repeated regularly. A starting rate of 82 becomes 83, then 83 becomes 85, and you're pretty much there.

Cadence improvement is best tackled in small five-minute blocks on your easy recovery runs. For a five-minute period, focus on improving your cadence by two strides per minute before resuming your normal run. Repeat this two to three times throughout your recovery run. If you repeat this process on every recovery run, then the improved cadence will start to filter over into the entirety of your recovery run and your normal run. It takes a focused effort, but it does happen.

A word of caution, however. The above is based on flat terrain. As you run hills your cadence will decrease relative to the gradient. It is important to try to keep cadence high, but there will come a crunch point for every runner when their cadence has dropped and their exertion (heart rate) is higher than they either want or are prepared to continue with. This is when you make the call to power walk, which is discussed at length later in this chapter.

HEAD FOR THE HILLS – RUN STRENGTH AND LONG-DISTANCE SPEED

Developing run strength is essential if you want to run well in an ultramarathon. You need to be strong – very strong! An ultramarathon is long, and the back third of the race is all about run strength. And run strength is all about the hills and vertical gain. In running, hills are the equivalent to lifting weights. Your body is the weight and your legs have to complete many repetitions to lift you up the hill. This provides a completely functional strength workout – it allows you to build the muscle fibres that are going to be needed if you want to run an ultramarathon.

For the ultra runner, whenever possible, your fartlek and interval runs should be completed on hills! You can often structure the workout by running towards the top of the hill and then turning and enjoying the run down. Such an approach has the effect of increasing the time spent running and has the fantastic benefit of using the hills to your advantage. You get a great workout on the way up the hill, and then, as your training progresses, you can use the downhills to your advantage as well by incorporating downhill efforts. This point can't be emphasised enough, and will be discussed in more depth shortly.

Hills are also the best way to build your long-distance speed. And this subject is important, because this is the area where many newbie ultra runners slip up (pardon the joke). As discussed earlier, you may have come from a half marathon and marathon background, which is fantastic, but running 42km on a nice, flat, sealed road and running 100km up hill and down dale are very different experiences. Critically, your top-end speed is not going to be you limiting factor when you complete your 100km ultra. Let's look more closely at why this is important.

As a quick exercise, work out your approximate expected run time for a 100km ultra. Now take off 30 minutes for aid stations (hopefully this is more than enough). Now calculate the following formula:

TIME (HOURS) X 60 = TIME TAKEN IN MINUTES

MINUTES TAKEN/100 = YOUR PACE PER KILOMETRE.

You'll see that your average pace for 100km is incredibly slow. Chances are you worked that number out twice because you thought you had made a mistake!

Top-end speed is not going to be your limiting factor. If you're still not convinced, here's an example based on a finish time of 12.5 hours:

12.5–0.5 = 12

12 X 60 = 720

720/100 = 7.2 (0.2 IS A 5TH OF A MINUTE, OR 12 SECONDS)

RACE PACE = 7.12 PACE/KM

For someone aiming for this time, this pace seems slow. Someone aiming for a sub 16-hour time, a 14-hour time or a sub 10-hour time will also have a pace that is relatively slow for them as an individual.

Race pace is surprisingly slow, and what this means with reference to the training program is that you don't need lots of fast reps; you need lots of longer distance reps at a lower speed. This helps build your muscular endurance. To intensify this, it helps if these longer reps can be completed uphill. The act of fighting gravity on each and every step intensifies the muscular endurance needed, so this type of a workout simultaneously works the body's muscular and energy systems.

I hope I've convinced you that, where possible, your long-distance speed training should be completed on hills. If not, remember that another benefit of training on hills is that there is a lower injury risk compared to running on a flat track. This is because running on a hill produces lower ground reaction forces (the force with which the foot strikes the ground) than running on the flat, where you will run at higher speeds because you don't have to fight gravity with each and every step.

If I still haven't convinced you that you need to do more long-distance speed training on hills, let's take a moment to visualise yourself on the start line. Are you there? Hear the birds, feel the mist in the air as you breathe, embrace the energy. At this point are you going to wish you had done more short-distance speed work, or are you going to be confident because you have done plenty of long-distance speed training on hills?

YOUR JOURNEY

Reflect on your current training and ask yourself:

- How many short intervals do you undertake?

- How many trail runs?

- How often do you run hills?

If you undertake lots of short intervals on large recoveries (i.e. flat 200, 400, 800m,) we are quickly going to obliterate them from your training program and include longer intervals. If you only run on trails once a week, you are ideally going to increase that to twice a week or more. And if you're not completing at least one of your intensity sets on hills, this will become your new aim. Of course, two would be better, but we understand that some ultra runners are confined to urban settings.

UPHILL TECHNIQUES

Runners often dread the uphills, but this certainly doesn't need to be the case. The first thing you need to do is accept the hill and accept that, regardless of your running ability, you're going to run slower when running uphill. Just because you slow down doesn't mean that you're not becoming a better runner through hill running. In fact, hills are great at training your runner physiology.

In addition to staying relaxed when running up hills, you need to make your cadence and stride length work for you. Let me explain why this is important by looking at how riding a bike uphill changes the required effort when you change gears. If you were to put your bike in a hard gear then try to ride up a hill, you would find that your cadence (in this case, how quickly your legs are spinning when cycling) would be really low. A low cadence places a huge demand on your musculoskeletal system; you need a great deal of strength. However, riding in such a fashion will not tax your cardiovascular system. If you ride up the hill again, but this time select the easiest gear possible, you will find that your cadence will be really high.

Your cardiovascular system will become 'maxed out' but your muscles – your musculoskeletal system – will not be working very hard. Exactly the same principles apply to running. And just as a bike has gears that you use when going uphill, so do you. These gears come in the form of your stride length.

So, how do we do it? We need to find balance. As discussed earlier, we need to keep our cadence when running at around 90 strides per minute, and we find this balance by changing our stride length. So, when running uphill your stride length will be much shorter than when running on the flat. Finding this balance will allow you to equally tax your cardiovascular system as well as your musculoskeletal system, thus allowing you to be as efficient and effective as possible when tackling the hill.

Depending on the steepness of the hill and your running ability, there can be a point when it's better to power hike (power walk) up the hill. The point at which this occurs is different for everyone, but you know you've hit that point when the cardiovascular effort required becomes exceedingly high despite having a short stride. It's hard work and you are going nowhere! At this point your progress up the hill will become faster and more efficient with a power hike. Power hiking is walking with purpose, but as we are still trying to make fast, efficient progress, there is a technique you should use. You need to lean forward at the waist and put your hands on your knees, which allows you to transfer your body weight from leg to leg to help 'power' you up the hill. You will also notice that when power hiking, the different technique allows you to increase your stride length.

Again, depending on the steepness of the hill and your ability, you may find you have to power hike the rest of the way to the top, or you may be able to intersperse periods of power hiking with running. This will all depend on the hill, the terrain and how you're feeling. This is something that you, personally, will have to experiment with to learn what works best for you.

Next time you're out running in the hills, have a play around with how you're running. Try a period with a lower cadence – how does that feel? Try a period with a higher cadence – how does that feel? Try power walking with the technique outlined above. Lastly, find the sweet spot between the two and enjoy the hill.

DOWNHILL TECHNIQUES

As the saying goes, what goes up must come down. This is the fun bit. What is often not recognised, though, is the physiological effect that downhill running can have on your fatigue levels. The uphills work the energy systems, but the downhills destroy the muscles, specifically your quads.

This is due to the 'eccentric loading' that is placed on your muscles when you run downhill. An eccentric load is a load that causes your muscles to work without changing their length. The best way to illustrate this is to get you to stand with your back against a wall. From there, gradually walk your legs out till your thighs are at a 90° angle to the wall and you're in a sitting position. Your back should still be against the wall. You are now in a position without any external support (i.e. no chair). In this position, you will find that your muscles are working really hard to support you; however, they are not changing in length. If you don't 'feel' it at first, just hold it for a little longer. This position forces your muscles to contend with large forces – the same type of force that they have to contend with when running downhill. The key point is that you need to take care when running down hills. Start gradually and build into them over a few weeks.

So how do we run down hills? Downhill running is all about your centre of gravity. If the hill is steep, you will have to keep your centre of gravity behind your feet. You are working to control, or decelerate, your mass as you proceed down the hill. This will cause you to go into somewhat of a 'sitting' position, in which you bring your arms up and out to the sides to help balance yourself. With this type of downhill running you will decrease your stride length and take frequent small steps, thus allowing greater contact time with the ground, which helps to keep you in control.

If the hill is only gradual and not technical, you will be able to maintain a more natural run technique. In this case your centre of gravity will be in front of your feet, thus allowing you to utilise gravity and accelerate down the hill. This is a complete contrast to the above. In this situation you will increase your stride length, your arms will be in, and in some instances you may even need to increase your cadence. Be careful when doing this – you don't want to end up out of control and taking a stack! Although, as I always say, we will have a laugh and then check you're okay – that's the rules. ☺

Often you will find that downhill runs require a mix of the above two running techniques. As your running ability improves, you will find that you're able to simultaneously switch between the two techniques to allow for the quickest passage down a hill. You'll be able to decelerate and keep yourself in control when the hill is steep or technical, then shift your centre of gravity forward to allow you to accelerate down the hill when the gradient decreases or the trail becomes less technical. The best bit: the only way to get better is to go and run the hills.

RACE SIMULATION

Race simulation occurs later in the ultra plan. The focus of these sets is to more closely mimic the demands of race day. A race simulation gives you a chance to practise everything required for race day. This way, if and when things go wrong, you can implement changes to ensure that these problems do not occur on your big day. Race simulation days allow you to ensure everything is in order, especially your nutrition, race pacing and gear. You're also likely to face additional challenges in such a set that you would not normally have to deal with. Understanding how to overcome these problems and challenges gives you confidence that, when faced with similar issues in a race, you will know what to do and how to cope. You will be able to say, 'I have been here before and know how to deal with this situation.' This will give you the ability to overcome the challenge and move on – fast.

・・ ・・ ・・ ・・

You now add to the mix an understanding of the specific long-distance training techniques that are used to train the ultra runner. You know how to utilise double run days and their extension, double run weekends. You understand that run strength is not only required, it is essential, over the final third of your race, and that running on hills is the best way to build this. You've got your head around more technical aspects of running such as cadence, and uphill and down-hill techniques. I've also convinced you that, as an ultra runner, the average pace you will hold for your race is much slower than what you're capable of running; top-end speed will not be your limiting factor on race day. You also know that uphill reps are best for developing your long-distance speed. Finally, you're aware of the importance of incorporating race simulation training into the overall plan, and can't wait to get started.

CHAPTER 8

PACING

Jane was excited as race day neared. She had all the usual nerves, but they were a good sign; they showed her that the race meant something. She knew she had done all of the hard work and had been running well for weeks. The training was in the bank! As she was standing on the start line, waiting for the gun to go, she was quietly confident that she could have a great race; one that her kids and husband would be proud of, one that *she* would be proud of.

As the gun went she started running. There was the sound of pounding all around, and she was swept up in the wave of excitement as all the runners charged off. She found her rhythm and settled in. As kilometre upon kilometre drifted by, she felt great – she was floating. This is how running and racing should be. Her watch hummed as the kilometres went by; she tried not to pay too much attention to the persistent shake on her wrist, but was delighted to know that she was well ahead of her goal time. She felt she could keep this up forever.

She kept running and savoured the moment, the freedom, the adrenaline – that feeling when your heart is beating hard in your chest and you know you're alive.

Then, almost suddenly, the feeling changed. What was happening? There was still a quarter of the race to go, and her legs were failing! She had been feeling great until now. 'Why are they failing me?' Jane thought. But she tried to reassure herself, 'I have built up a buffer so it's not too bad, I'll still be able to make my goal time.'

To her dismay, her pace slowed and other runners started to pass her. She simply couldn't fight it; mentally she was giving it her all, but her pace just kept dropping. She struggled on, the finish line now in sight. When she finally crossed it, she slumped in a pile, exhausted and disappointed. She had done all of the training, she knew she was fit and she had been in front of her time. So what had happened?

What had happened was that her pacing was off. Pacing is one of the most under-valued skills in ultra running, yet it's essential for success at any level and any distance; for runners competing in local trail and ultra races right through to experienced athletes competing at big international events. It is essential for every runner: beginner, intermediate, advanced, and even the elite. You must have this skill if you want to make it to the finish line of your 100km ultramarathon. Working on and developing your pacing prowess can bring huge results, including personal bests and a much higher sense of satisfaction when you cross the finish line. You not only know you have run well, you also know that you have given it your all.

However, while a sound understanding of your personal pacing can deliver these results, pacing is not an improvement in fitness. It works with what you're already capable of doing. I love tapping into this latent potential with the trail and ultra runners I work with. It delivers improved results without an improvement in fitness, but, as pacing knowledge increases, training sets improve and consequently fitness improves at a quicker rate as well. It's a win/win! And the best news? You can do it too!

So what is this elusive thing called pacing? Pacing is the ability to control your exertion over a period of time. To accept that pacing is important, we need to agree that the average pace per kilometre that you're capable of holding is quicker for a 1km dash than it is for a 5km trail run. Similarly, the pace you can hold for a 5km run is quicker than it is for a full marathon and, especially, an ultramarathon.

PACING AND THE BODY

As an ultra runner you need a comprehensive understanding of pacing. This is the best way, physiologically, to deliver your personal best result. Let me put this in simple terms. Because of the way the body functions, two things happen if you overshoot in your running. First, you push your energy systems too far. This means that they need to have a period of recovery before you can return to a sustainable level. Second, you 'damage' your muscles. This is actually what you do when training, and is what helps you build strength – when the muscles recover, they come back stronger. However, this recovery takes days, and in a race you don't have time for this to happen. Muscle damage equates to fatigue, so if you get your pacing wrong when racing, it equates to an exponential loss of time over the second half of your ultra. To sum up, if you overshoot your energy systems, you need to back off to allow yourself to recover. If you overshoot for a prolonged period relative to your race distance (100km), then you accumulate too much fatigue (muscle damage) early, and this causes you to slow exponentially over the reminder of the race.

You may have heard people talk about the famed negative split. This is when you run the second half of the race quicker than the first half of your race. And it's not all that hard to achieve if you go in with a pacing plan, as discussed below. If, however, you go in without a plan of action, then a negative split is exceedingly hard to achieve. Good pacing builds in a safeguard that allows you to have a great race every time. It gives you enough structure to put you in a position to have a great race, but also allows you the freedom to run faster and exceed your goal when it counts.

HOW TO ACHIEVE PERSONAL PACING PROWESS

So how do you go about achieving this negative split? There are two things you need to do:

1. Practise pacing in training.

2. Have a pacing plan when you race.

The key to the pacing plan is to break your race into thirds; however, over time it has become apparent that this works a little better if these thirds are slightly skewed. This is easier to explain with examples of races shorter than an ultramarathon, and let's also assume that these races are fairly flat compared to typical ultramarathons and trail races. Once you understand the concept, we can apply it to trail races, ultra races and, of course, your 100km ultra.

So, what this looks like for the **HALF MARATHON** is an 8km chunk, a second 8km chunk and a final 5km chunk. Your aim is to run the first 8km at goal-race pace plus five seconds per kilometre. For the middle chunk, you drop your pace down to goal-race pace. Then for the final chunk, you bring it home with everything that you have left, ideally goal-race pace less five or more seconds per kilometre.

You might be doing the maths and thinking, 'This means I'm going to be fifteen seconds off my goal pace.' In a strict sense this is the case; however, this strategy has the potential to allow you to exceed, if not obliterate, your PB. Chances are that over the final 5km, you're going to be feeling great and will be more than five seconds per kilometre under your race pace. If you're not, then your aim is just to hold your expected race pace through to the finish, which still allows you to have a fantastic race based on what you are truly capable of.

For the **MARATHON**, a pacing plan follows the same concept and breaks the race up into chunks of 15km, 15km and 12km. Again, the first 15km is at race pace plus five seconds per kilometre, the middle 15km is at goal-race pace, while the last 12km is at race pace less five seconds or more per kilometre.

Interestingly, this means that you should hit the 30km mark feeling great (well, as great as you can, having just banked 30km at a steady clip). When everyone else hits struggle town you'll be in your groove, hitting the afterburners and flying for home. Watch as you pass all those people who had a poor pacing strategy. Winning!

This same concept applies to **TRAIL AND ULTRA RACES**; however, things are a little more complex. The plan is still to aim to follow a similar method to the one discussed above. So, for a 30km trail race, your pacing would be broken up into 11km, 11km and 8km segments. However, the inconsistent terrain that you're likely to face will make things tricky. Generally, the uphill and downhill segments will cause the biggest discrepancy, and you need to be aware that hills will force you to throw times 'out the window'. So instead of aiming for times, aim for a feeling. You should feel in control for the first section, steady for the second section and run hard in the final section. This is where RPE becomes vital, and why practising pacing in training is important – it teaches you how to know and understand what your goal intensity 'feels' like.

When developing a pacing plan for an **ULTRAMARATHON** of, say, 100km (who would have thought!), we need to follow the same method. Break the race up into chunks of 35km, 35km and 30km. We need to start easy and build into things over the race. As fatigue builds, you may find that you're only capable of holding your initial easy pace, but suddenly that feels a lot harder. Fatigue is going to happen to everyone, so what you have to do is prevent these fatigue levels rising too quickly. If fatigue levels rise too quickly you may find that you don't make it to the finish or are left having to slow your running drastically or even walk.

A pacing plan accepts that fatigue is going to occur but keeps you in a great position by preventing it from rising too quickly, allowing you the freedom to run faster when it counts. Patience, patience, patience.

YOUR JOURNEY

While you now have a pacing plan in place, good pace control won't just happen come race day. You need to practise it in training. You can practise pace control in almost any set, and below are a few examples. Always complete an appropriate warm-up before a set, and a suitable cool down afterwards.

For the **HALF MARATHON** or trail race of an equivalent time to your road half marathon, complete the following main set. Divide the set into three 10-minute blocks – 10/10/10 – and pace yourself as follows:

- Block 1 – race pace plus 5 seconds per km
- Block 2 – goal-race pace
- Block 3 – race pace less 5 seconds per km.

Complete the 10/10/10 segments straight through, programming them into your watch or hitting the lap key between sections. This mimics what you will undertake on race day when your blocks would be 8km, 8km and 5km chunks.

For the **MARATHON** or equivalent-timed trail race (i.e. cumulative time equivalent to cumulative road marathon time) follow the same concept, but move the blocks out to 15 minutes or even 20 minutes. So the set becomes 15/15/15 or 20/20/20. Pace yourself as follows:

- Block 1 – goal marathon pace less 5 seconds per km
- Block 2 – goal marathon pace
- Block 3 – goal marathon pace less 5 seconds per km.

Complete the 15/15/15 or 20/20/20 segments straight through, programming them into your watch or hitting the lap key between sections.

As there are both short and longer trail races, the intensity of the set should mirror race day, but be completed on terrain similar to your target race. In other words, if your trail race is shorter in terms of time (not distance), choose the set from above that best matches your cumulative finish time. (Is the time spent running approximate to your half marathon or your full marathon?) Choose whichever is closest and complete the appropriate set from above.

While the above examples provide great ways to practise pacing in higher intensity training sets, the following set is something that we recommend you undertake on a long run to help your prepare for your **100KM ULTRA** race.

Divide your set into three 40-minute blocks – 40/40/40 – and pace yourself as follows.[18]

- Block 1 – easy
- Block 2 – steady
- Block 3 – hard (but don't go over the top, this is a two-hour set, and when you tackle your 100km ultra you will be running for much longer than this. If you start to feel the signs of fatigue after two hours, consider how that would play out exponentially over another eight or more.)

With this set, we recommend completing a 60-second walk between sections. Aim to keep the 60-second walk separate from the 40-minute running blocks. This allows you to compare the average pace achieved in each block without it being skewed by the 60-second walk. Keep in mind that a change in terrain can, and likely will, affect your average pace for each segment. One way to combat this is to complete segments over the same course, such as three mini loops.

As you get closer to your race, you can gradually increase the length of the 40-minute segments to one hour. This will create a continuing challenge and begin to more accurately match the demands of race day, both in terms of the time and the energy demands required. This set would look like this:

---

18   Keep in mind that this is a long set and, depending on where your personal running is currently at, you may need to build up to this.

- 60 minutes, easy
- 60 minutes, steady
- 60 minutes, hard.

Completing one-hour loops over the same course is a fantastic way to determine your pacing control and start to fully appreciate the effects of fatigue on the body. At the conclusion of the set, compare the average heart rate and pace for each segment. Comparing your first lap to your last lap often provides the most interesting comparison. Correlating the data with how you *feel* or *felt* can provide the best insight about your personal pacing. From this point, you can refine and practise your pacing in subsequent runs.

PACING YOUR 100KM ULTRA USING ZONES

Now think back to Chapter 3 and what you learnt about intensity and zones. Remember that combining heart rate and RPE gives you the best guide to your pace. When this is combined with an understanding that fatigue builds over the entirety of a race, it places you in a position to ensure you nail this critical element. You need to break your race up into skewed thirds of 35/35/30. The exact feel and intensity that you're capable of holding is unique to each ultra runner and must be practised in training – ideal pacing won't just happen.

As a guide, for the first third of your 100km ultra, you need to operate in Zone 1/2 and be wary of allowing your heart rate to drift into Zone 3, even on the hills. To clarify, if you're expecting a finish time *under* 12 hours, then aim for Zone 2; if you're expecting a finish time *over* 12 hours, aim to keep it in Zone 1 and low Zone 2. For the middle third, aim to keep your heart rate consistent at these levels; however, you can expect the effort required to maintain this level to increase dramatically.

This leaves you with your final third to go. By this stage you will have a very good understanding of what you're capable of. In this stage you can either look to maintain this pattern through to the end or, if you feel you have gas left in the tank, you can look to increase your effort over the final third of the race. By this stage, you will be able to make educated and informed decisions about what you're capable of. You will increase your pace when it counts, and pass all those who went out too hard at the start and had a poor pacing strategy. Even though you'll be in the hurt locker, imagine how great you're going to feel as you pass all those people!

You are now equipped with the knowledge required to improve your race pacing and your pacing in training. If you find it difficult at first, don't worry, that just demonstrates that you have more to gain than someone who nails it the first time. Don't be disheartened and stick with it – it just takes practice. And that just means more running, which certainly can't be a bad thing, right?

The two things you are going to commit to are:

1. Practising a pacing set at least once in your training. Make sure you review your data afterwards to see how you went.

2. Leading into your next race, you are going to go in with a pacing plan as outlined above, following the rule of skewed thirds. Try it at least once; you will be surprised at what you're capable of!

You now have a firm understanding that pacing in an essential technique that requires mastery by the ultra athlete. You understand that you can push both your energy systems and your fatigue level too far and too early in a training set or race. This is detrimental to your overall goal, as it can cause you to exponentially slow over the final part of your race. You understand that to combat this you need to hit a negative split. Having a pacing plan that you can implement will ensure this occurs. You're also aware that this won't just happen by magic, but that you need to practise this in training. You need to undertake a range of training sets so that you can practise and refine your pacing to ensure that you master it. Knowledge and understanding is one thing, but implementation is another, so you best get out there running. Next, in Part 3, we bring everything together and develop your body into a long-distance weapon!

PERFECT PREPARATION

Imagine having your perfect ultramarathon.

As you run, the uphills are effortless, the downhills enjoyable. You're moving freely as the fast single track disappears beneath your feet. You flow with the trail, thinking, 'Wow, it's great to be out running.' Everything is going perfectly: you're floating, you're fast, you're in the moment and you're free.

Now let's take it a bit further. You've finished the race and achieved a long-cherished dream. What is that dream? Maybe it was to finish your first 100km ultramarathon, maybe it was to run further than you ever had before, maybe it was the first step in a transformation to an ultra runner lifestyle and a new you!

But it doesn't have to be just a dream. If you make your dream a goal, you have the power to make it come true by focusing on what you do between now and that perfect race. You are capable of achieving your dream; and this, the final part of this book, will show you how to do that!

Of course, there is no guarantee that you will get everything perfect the first time, every time. You will make mistakes. That's no problem at all – that's called learning and it's all part of the journey. But if you give it a go, the worst thing that can happen is that you will improve, and that's certainly not a bad thing.

One good run won't improve your fitness at all. One good week of running will do little to improve your fitness. There is no magical set. It's consistent commitment to your ultra running program, over a prolonged period of time, that will deliver results. Long-term consistency is the cornerstone, but it's also vital that you do the right 'work' as it relates to your end goal.

This section is where all the knowledge you have been exposed to comes together. The first part of preparing for your race is about gathering your team. You then go on and make sure you've got your gear properly sorted.

Then, after understanding some key principles, we'll get to the hard-core stuff. You will see how an ultra running program is structured; this includes the short, middle and long-term plans. You will see how and why a taper is needed, and how recovery is included within an ultra running program. Finally you will tackle your big dance, your big day: race day. You will have concerns but they will be covered in detail. The questions that you may not have thought about yet, the ones that come up at the last minute, they will be covered. No stone will be left unturned. You will finish this book confident that when you front the start line for your first 100km ultramarathon, you will be prepared and will make the finish line.

CHAPTER 9

GATHER YOUR TEAM

When embarking upon the journey of training for your first 100km ultramarathon, you need to be aware that while the final effort may be a solo endeavour, there is a team of people behind the scenes who play vital roles in enabling you to stand at the start line and feel confident about the task ahead.

Without this team in place you face an increased risk of injury, and are in danger of using your training time poorly and missing training sets. You might find yourself with a body that is beat up and a life that's out of balance. People often look to the 'pros' and think, 'But they're able to achieve this all on their own!' Not true. The pro's use a team better than anyone. Take Olympic great Anna Meares, for example, who is a multiple Olympic gold medallist, won medals at four consecutive Olympic Games and has been Australian Olympic team captain – and that's just scratching the surface of her achievements! She has a coach, mentors, a physiotherapist and a masseuse on her team, and she also has a supportive family. Sure, they may not be paraded front and centre and may not get a mention in public, but they are there behind the scenes doing their jobs. Every elite-level football team also has support staff on hand. Why? Because it enhances the individual's, and consequently the team's, chance of success.

Having a team in place makes the journey more rewarding and allows you to achieve your impossible dream.

With a little bit of knowledge, it's not hard for you to implement the same approach that professionals use, and watch your ability to achieve your 100km ultra skyrocket. How we go about achieving this is through working with independent providers, each of whom specialise in one area. So let's discuss the people on your team, why you need them and how to ensure they're playing a pivotal role in your race preparation.

THE SUPPORTIVE FAMILY – YOUR CLOSEST ALLY

The first group you need on your side is your family. This is especially important if there are dependent kids involved, or if you plan on completing more than one ultra. You need to include these critical people in your journey. If they're not involved, they may end up resenting your running and feel that it detracts from the family-life balance – they'll think your running is taking you away from them. If the family feels this way about your running, they may push back against you and your beloved sport. This resentment can cause your family to make training more challenging than it already is, and can make you feel alone in your endeavour. You certainly don't want that. However, if you take a few steps to involve your family in your journey, they can become an active part of it. They will enjoy what your running brings to family life, and encourage and support you more than you ever anticipated.

So how do you go about ensuring that your family supports you? You need to involve them. They need to feel a part of the journey towards your achievement, but without finding their role onerous.

Each family and their individual life and work commitments are different, but there are many and varied ways to involve the family in your ultra journey – especially your training. The following list provides a starting point:

- If you're running on the road or trail, choose paths that are appropriate for bikes so the kids can ride with you. As they get older, they will be able to outride you and will be capable of tackling trails of increasing difficulty. They can also be great water carriers.

- Mix your training up once in a while so that your big run day doesn't fall on the weekend. This can be achieved in a number of ways, such as double run days. This gives you more time with the family on the weekend; something they will thank you for.

- If you always run in the morning, change it to an afternoon run once a month so that you're around in the morning and can spend time with the kids or your partner.

- Organise for the family to meet you for coffee after your run. This can be a great way to complete a point-to-point run rather than a looped course, as you conveniently now have a lift back.

- Let the kids know that running is something that is really important for you, but ask them if there's something special they would like to do, such as playing mini golf, going to a movie, playing at the beach or visiting a new park. Make sure you keep your promise and treat them to the outing they want when you're back from your run. This helps kids to associate your running with quality, fun family time.

- Encourage your partner to run or walk. If they're new to running, they may have to come on one of your easy runs, or alternatively aim to finish at the same time and place for coffee.

- Make a weekend of it and camp (or glamp, if that's your style) at national parks. This allows you to find new trails.

People regularly underestimate the importance of having the family on side with their running, but by involving them in your journey it increases the enjoyment and fun for all. And the best bit? Running is priceless, free, family fun!

YOUR JOURNEY

Over the next two weeks, make sure to include your partner or kids in your running at least once. Make sure to unlock the fun and feel the meaning that running brings to your lives.

Now let's discuss the professionals you need.

THE ULTRA COACH – FAST-TRACKING YOUR SUCCESS

The first professional to put into your corner is a coach – someone who has been there before and understands how to guide you on your journey. This is important, as this guidance will allow you to invest your training time where it's most beneficial. Through their knowledge and expertise, a coach is able to guide you to achieving your desired results more quickly. This allows you to unlock goals you never before thought possible. An informal survey run by Training Peaks found the top seven reasons athletes liked to work with a coach were: accountability, structure, smarts, reduced risk of over-training, motivation, time management, and finally but importantly, so 'they don't have to do the thinking'.[19] Collectively, these factors combine to give runners who are coached greater improvement, and increased improvement rates, than those who aren't. Moreover, there are risks if you don't put a coach in your corner. These include DNFs, DNSs, injuries, dwindling motivation and a failure to see the big picture about what you're trying to achieve.

But despite the obvious benefits of working with a coach, ultra runners often find that taking this step takes them out of their comfort zone. Regular comments include:

- I'm not good enough!

- No one would want to work with me!

- I'm just not comfortable working with a coach.

- It wouldn't benefit me.

These are all excuses used to avoid the uncomfortable feeling of taking that first step and contacting a coach. However, it's often the athletes who are most reluctant to work with a coach who, after finally taking the plunge, can't imagine ultra running without one. They love being coached by a professional and the benefits it brings.

---

19   https://www.trainingpeaks.com/blog/the-top-7-reasons-to-work-with-a-coach/

CHOOSING A COACH

There are three ways that you can take action in this important area. The first is to find a local or online ultramarathon coach, and I highly recommended this. Whether it's joining my community at The Ultra Journey or engaging another local or online ultra coach, there are three essentials to look for before you employ someone:

1. You have to believe in their coaching philosophy.

2. They need to believe in you as the athlete.

3. The coach-athlete relationship has to gel so that you can function as a team.

This is likely to seem pretty straightforward, and it is, except when it doesn't work.

At this point it's important that I share a story from my past. Since being a younger athlete and through to today, I have had many coaches (I believe it's important for everyone to receive professional coaching, even a coach). I once had an exceptional coach, whom I decided to work with so he could help me achieve my endurance goals. Although his coaching philosophy was on song with mine, I enjoyed his training sets and he believed in me as an athlete, we just didn't gel. Needless to say, a few months later we both went our separate ways. One of the three essential ingredients was missing: we simply couldn't function as a unit.

Sometimes this lack of cohesion will be apparent immediately, in which case you should walk away immediately. Other times this lack of cohesion will not be immediately apparent, as was the case for me. After making contact with a coach and finding your initial conversations all go well, you'll find that the athlete-coach relationship will still take time to build. Over the first four to eight weeks the coach is learning about how you function as an athlete, and you're learning about how the coach likes to operate. If the coach-athlete relationship doesn't feel right after this time, don't be afraid to (politely) walk away and find another coach.

I will be the first to say that I am not the perfect coach for every ultra runner, nor am I going to enjoy working with every ultra runner. No coach is right for every athlete and no athlete is right for every coach. I'll also let you in on a secret here – if it's not working for you, it's not working for your coach! I am proactive in this matter, but not all coaches are, so don't be afraid to cut the ties if it's not working and make sure you find a perfect match.

If the cost of hiring a professional ultra run coach is prohibitive, then your next option is to find an ultra running mentor. Someone you know and trust, and who has achieved goals similar to yours. Much like a coach, they can provide a unique perspective. Other runners are normally more than happy to pass on their knowledge, and they also make great training partners. Do be careful, however, to select the 'right' mentor. While you may think you can find one among your best friends, and find someone who means well, there is a lot of misinformation out there and you could be putting your trust in someone who's not really keen or up to the job. So make sure their apparent knowledge really is what it's reputed to be by asking about their experience. And don't think your friends will be offended if you look outside your immediate circle for a mentor –sometimes this is the best way to find a mentor with the appropriate perspective on your situation.

Lacking someone who might be a suitable mentor, the final option you have is to join a local run group or run club. The regularity and structure provided by running with a group is great, as it yields a huge source of motivation and allows you to meet like-minded individuals. But a word of warning! Be careful with the run group you select, as ultra running is different from road and track running. In the past I have seen athletes join run groups not well suited to their goals. For ultra runners, the local trail run group is often the best place to start.

We want you to be open to the idea of hiring an ultra coach or working with an ultra coaching program, but today we are simply planting a seed and opening your mind to the possibilities of fast-tracking your progress. After you have finished reading this book, you will be in a more powerful position to know what you are after when it comes to an ultra coach.

THE PHYSIOTHERAPIST – PREVENTION, NOT CURE!

The next person you need in your team is the physiotherapist.[20] This person is essential to your team. Now, you might be thinking, 'But I'm not going to get injured!' But I don't want you to think cure, I want you to think prevention and improved performance. The first time you see your physiotherapist should be *before* you start running

---

20   Some people prefer the chiropractor, osteopath, etc. For this book I am not going to enter that debate, I am going to go with physiotherapist, but you may choose your appropriate professional.

or, more likely in your case, before increasing your training load. Why? Let me explain.

You need to understand what is often referred to as the 'injury window'. This period occurs three to four weeks after you start running, increase your training load, or return from injury or illness. The body can absorb the increased load easily enough for a while, but suddenly, at this three to four-week mark – boom! Your body finally breaks. This can occur for a number of reasons, but the most common are:

- Increasing the run load too quickly (how much or how fast you're running each week).

- A muscle imbalance.

- A limited range of motion.

When injury strikes, all that motivation you had and all that fitness you put in place is gone in an instant. But if we take the prevention course, we anticipate potential injury and put steps in place to ensure it doesn't occur.

This simply means two things: a structured approach to increasing your run load, and booking in to see your local physiotherapist for an exercise pre-screen. Your physiotherapist will be able to tell if you're fundamentally weak in any particular area, or if you have a limited range of motion that needs to be rectified. They will give you the guidance to solve the problem and get you on your way.

Stan Garland, a physio guru who has worked around the world, assisted Olympians and elite athletes from numerous sporting codes, and worked with weekend warriors as well as countless runners, states that:

An exercise pre-screen has the ability to not only decrease your chances of injury but also increase your performance, as you are now able to recruit the appropriate muscles required for efficient running.

The other time your physiotherapist is going to be your best friend is when you get a 'niggle'. There is a difference between 'sore from running', a.k.a. fatigue, and 'injury pain'. Learning this difference is important. If and when you recognise any potential injury signs, be proactive rather than reactive – book yourself in for an appointment. It's tough for runners to accept, but three days off running now is better than three months off later – just think about how grumpy you would be about the latter!

Stan recommends booking in to see a physio if any of the following signs are present:

- Niggles that are persistent, i.e. three days plus. Any longer than a week and you risk interrupting your long-term consistency.

- Unusually sore muscles.

- Sharp pains.

CHOOSING A PHYSIO

If you don't have a physiotherapist, I would encourage you to ask or search for the following information before enlisting their services. If you already have a physiotherapist, mentally check that they tick these boxes:

- Can three runners (preferably more) recommend their services and results?

- Do they have a personal interest in running or in team sports that involve extensive running?

The second point is essential. Time and time again runners start with a 'generic' physiotherapist, who doesn't truly appreciate what they do – even in sports physiotherapy circles running an ultra is not considered normal! You need someone on your team who understands running.

YOUR JOURNEY

Ask around your local running circles and find a physiotherapist who works with runners. Book in and organise an athletic pre-screen to help identify problems that may come up as you increase your running. Then take the steps outlined by the physiotherapist to prevent these problems from occurring. If you walk away after your appointment with no concerns, this is fantastic – you can feel even more confident about what you're about to tackle!

THE REMEDIAL MASSAGE THERAPIST

A car needs a service, and so do your muscles. The final professional to put in your team is the remedial massage therapist. I'm not talking the light fluffy stuff here, I'm talking about a deep tissue massage that provides relief for muscles that have been working hard. The training you will be undertaking on a weekly basis means that regular massage is imperative to keeping you free of injury and running freely.

According to remedial massage therapist Michael Fildes, who has worked with the likes of Rohan Dennis (Tour de France stage winner and Olympic medallist) and Jenni Screen (Olympic basketball champion), as well as elite Australian Rules footballers:

The benefits of massage are outstanding. When someone hops on the table for a massage I can always tell by the feel of their muscles if they have regular massage or not; the difference is quite astounding. When you are exercising you are causing your muscles and the surrounding tissues to tighten up. By having a deep tissue massage we can help to break up the toxins and elements that have accumulated that make you feel tighter.

Ideally, ultra runners should be getting a massage every one to two weeks, but this is not possible for many. However, it's recommended that you book in at least every three to four weeks for a remedial massage. The volume of running that you're tackling means that you need to keep on top of things rather than let problems develop, which makes it much harder to solve them. As Mike says, 'The deep tissue massage will help to keep your body softer and more flexible as it will help remove those toxins.'

CHOOSING A MASSAGE THERAPIST

Finding a good remedial massage therapist can be difficult. Mike suggests runners use the following questions to find out if the masseuse will be high value. If they don't provide a great deep tissue massage, don't be afraid to move on until you find one who does.

• Can you describe to me the type of massage technique you use and how you physically work on clients?

- What other sports people do you work on and what type of sport do they participate in?

- What benefits can I expect as a result of your remedial massage?

- How regularly do you perform deep tissue massage?

YOUR JOURNEY

This one is easy. Find an appropriate remedial massage therapist and book an appointment within the next fortnight – no cancelling! While you may not completely enjoy the massage, you will enjoy the results.

THE DOCTOR – GET A MEDICAL PRE-SCREEN

While they do not form part of your ongoing team, visiting your regular doctor for a medical pre-screen is always recommended prior to undertaking a specific ultra running program.

⸱⸳ ⸳⸱ ⸱⸳ ⸳⸱

Now you know the team that you need around you to increase your chances of success on your ultra journey. You know who you need on your team and why each of these people is essential. You understand that elite-level athletes, and sporting teams, have these professionals (and others) in place to help ensure their success, and so must you.

To recap, your team members are:

- The supportive family – your closest ally

- The ultra coach – fast-tracking your success

- The physiotherapist – prevention, not cure
- The remedial massage therapist – a car needs servicing, so do your muscles.

You need to be proactive in putting each of these helpers in place. You want not just a good team, but a great team. Their support will become increasingly important as you progress on your ultra journey.

CHAPTER 10

GET YOUR GEAR

Gear, gear, gear, gear! Runners love gear! The next step in your race preparation is to make sure you have the right gear to get you through 100km. Of course, you need to have the right gear during your training as well, and training also provides a way of testing your gear to make sure it'll work the way you want it to on your big day. I'm going to go through the essentials so that you have the right gear to improve your ultra running experience. This will be an unbiased cut through the jargon to look at the important stuff. We are going to look at shoes, run packs, jackets, watches and mandatory gear.

First some general principles. You should not even know that your gear is there, it should form an extension of your body. Do you think about your running shoes when running? Generally you're looking at the birds, the trees, the trail, the koalas – not your shoes! Until you start to get sore feet… You will only start to think about gear when it's not performing its function and causing you problems. So let's make sure you get the right gear.

It's also important to do some trial and error! This is because everybody has personal preferences, and different body shapes and running styles suit different gear. Especially with footwear and socks, as people's feet are all very different! As long as you understand the function of the product and what to look for, as opposed to lis-

JOURNEY TO 100

tening to the marketing hype, then the job's done; you are now an informed consumer making informed decisions.

SHOES

A common question asked by those new to trail and ultra running is: can I wear my road shoes on the trails? While we certainly can't stop you, we recommend purchasing a trail-specific pair of shoes. Your road running shoes are simply not designed to withstand the demands of trail running. Road shoes are built and function incredibly well for the demands of road running, and this is the activity they were designed to undertake. So rather than beat up your road shoes on the trails, purchase a pair of trail-specific shoes and keep your road shoes for the road; it's much cheaper in the long run. In fact, you will easily cover the distance in training that justifies buying a couple of pairs of trail shoes.

The specific differences between a trail and road shoe include:

- More durable fabrics to support the foot and allow the shoe to cope with the rugged terrain. This often makes trail running shoes slightly heavier than road running shoes.

- More aggressive soles to ensure traction on the trail.

- More lateral (side to side) support to cope with the unique demands of trail running.

- Wider soles to help prevent the foot rolling on uneven ground.

- Rock plate. Trail shoes often have a firm plate between the sole on the bottom of the shoe and the midsole. This allows for the

154

force of treading on trail debris – in particular, sharp rocks to be dispersed rather than focused on one point of your foot.

- Toecap. Trail shoes feature a toecap to prevent the toes being injured if you kick rocks, stairs or other debris when running.

WATCHES AND TRACKING DEVICES

Runners love to track things, especially kilometres or miles! The GPS watch and heart rate monitor have revolutionised training. As running power-meters improve they may be the next revolution, but the mammoth breakthrough for trail and ultra running will come with real-time blood lactate monitoring that is reported to your watch. While the technology for this is in development, its commercial availability and accuracy are still a few years off. What draws all these components together is that this information is displayed through a watch. And runners love their watches! While we don't want to underestimate the fun and benefit of simply donning the shoes and going out for a run, we are aware that almost all of you are going to use a watch.

If you're in the market for a watch the following functions are most critical for the ultra runner:

- Time
- Heart rate
- GPS – distance
- Cadence
- Elevation
- A long battery life.

Most of these are becoming standard today, but the one feature that is really beneficial to ultra runners – elevation – is currently not standard on every watch.

As for brands, this comes down to personal preference. Sunnto, Garmin and Polar are the biggest brands and all offer high-quality watches that will meet all the above needs. Go with what you like the look of or what fits your price point.

As my friends over at Training Peaks say, 'What gets measured gets done.' But the watch is only half of this equation. There are various ways to track your training. The traditional approach was to record your training in a diary, but as technology has improved, online options such as Strava, Garmin Connect or Training Peaks make this easier, more efficient and fun. It is recommended that when you purchase your watch, you link it to an existing account or set up a personal account on your chosen platform.

WEIGHT VS. DURABILITY

For the remaining items in this chapter, the weight vs. durability debate comes into play. Fortunately the technology available has dramatically decreased the weight of the items you are required to carry as part of your mandatory gear list. This weight reduction has come about through the development of improved fabrics and run-specific gear that is minimalist in nature. These improvements mean that these items come at a premium price. However, in my view these items are worth the additional outlay in order to save weight on the trails.

YOUR JOURNEY

To gauge the effect that an additional one kilo has on your run pace, on one of your long runs fill your pack with an unnecessary litre of water and carry it for your journey. You will quickly appreciate the additional effort that carrying an extra kilo of water creates. This is no different from carrying an additional kilo of gear. Light is fast.

RUNNING PACKS

When it comes to carrying your gear, nutrition and hydration, a pack is incredibly important. Due to the vertical movement created when running, a run-specific pack, sometimes called a vest pack, is essential. The pack needs to conform to the shape of your back and you should keep the heaviest items – your water or fluids (sports drink) – as close to your centre of mass as possible. This means holding these items firmly against your back. To allow this conforming fit and comfort, run packs are quite soft and malleable. When you need to carry extra fluid, a run-specific pack is particularly useful. Fluid can be stored on each of the shoulder straps, in specific bottles, thus keeping the weight more evenly distributed.

In contrast, a daypack or even lightweight hiking pack often has a more rigid construction. The purpose of this is to keep uncomfortable items from pressing into the back and transfer their weight to the hips. But when you wear this type of pack while running you feel the items move from side to side on your back, creating an uncomfortable running experience.

Beyond this there are different size run packs available. As a rule of thumb you should aim to take the most minimal pack that meets the load carrying needs of your event. For most 100km races a water carrying capacity of two litres is needed, along with additional storage of 12–15 litres for the required mandatory gear. Again there is a range of brands on the market. The best bet is to borrow a few different packs from friends to see what you find most comfortable before making a purchase.

RAIN JACKETS

Rain jackets perform two functions, the obvious one being to keep the rain off. The other is to keep the wind out. The first concept that you need to understand is that when you put a jacket on you're placing a barrier between your skin and the outside air. This means that there is a barrier that your sweat (water vapour) has to pass through before it gets to the open air. Regardless of the type of jacket, there is now a barrier preventing your sweat from escaping. When you're running you are exercising hard and often producing more sweat than you realise.

To help this sweat escape you will hear people and manufacturers talk about 'breathability'. This is the ability of the fabric to allow moisture to pass through it. Water in a droplet form (rain) is much larger than it is in a vapour form (sweat). Raindrops are too large to get through minuscule holes in the fabric, so it beads and runs off. However, sweat is small enough to escape through these teeny tiny holes. The more of these little holes in the fabric, the more 'breathable' the fabric is said to be. At the end of the day, however, there is still a barrier between your skin and the outside air, so you will likely still find some moisture on the inside of the jacket after you have been running in it, despite the fabric being very breathable. To give yourself a contrast of the difference between a high-quality jacket and a low-quality jacket you could purchase a cheap poncho (rain jacket with no breathability) and run in it for a while. You will soon see a very real difference. Now convinced that you need a high-quality jacket, the additional determining factors are fit, weight, cost and what you like the look of!

WOOL VS. SYNTHETIC FABRIC

Another common concern for ultra runners is the wool vs. synthetic debate. Both provide distinct benefits *and* disadvantages, and knowing this it's simply a matter of deciding which option is best for your personal needs and preferences. The benefits of synthetic are that the fabrics are comparatively cheap to make and are lighter in comparison to wool products. Their drawback is that they can get pongy (smelly) much quicker than wool, so if you don't anticipate being able to wash them after each run, this can become a concern. The benefit of wool is that it breaths better, i.e. it works more closely with your body temperature. It's also important to mention that both products will keep you warm when wet, unlike cotton, which will not trap the heat. However, wool will be much heavier when wet as it is more absorbent and holds a lot more moisture than a synthetic product. As a result it really comes down to personal preference as to which product will meet your individual needs.

I personally use synthetic products when running, due to their lighter weight – both dry and when wet – and cheaper price. And I don't find their inability to match my body temperature an issue.

By comparison, if I'm out hiking or walking around the city, I opt for wool products. You will have to select what's right for your personal trail needs.

ADDITIONAL MANDATORY GEAR

Mandatory gear is the stuff you *have* to take on your ultra, even if you don't want to. The mandatory gear list will vary with each race; however, as a guide it will include the following items:

- Race bib
- Race timing tag (sometimes on the back of the race bib)
- Long sleeve thermal top
- Long leg thermal pants
- Waterproof and breathable jacket
- Long leg waterproof pants
- Lightweight fleece
- Beanie
- Full-fingered lightweight gloves
- Headlamp
- Water bottles or water bladders
- Emergency space blanket
- Spare back-up light
- Compass
- Whistle
- Mobile phone

- High visibility safety vest
- Map
- Waterproof matches
- Blister pads – this is one item that you should always pack, even if you don't think you will need them.

The race organisers will supply some of these, i.e. race bib, timing tag and often a map, but it's best to check your event website or competitor book for the exact requirements.

. . . .

You are now equipped with the necessary knowledge to purchase the gear you need to be comfortable on the trail and to help ensure you enjoy running in all conditions. More importantly, you've had a run-down on the mandatory gear you'll need heading into your race, and know that you need to practise running in your gear to ensure a comfortable race day. The next step in your perfect preparation is to understand the planning principles that will underpin your training program.

CHAPTER 11

UNDERSTAND PLANNING

Now that you've got your support team in place and have been on your shopping spree and you're all kitted out in your new running gear, I bet you're dying to lock in a training plan and start working it. But you need to be patient for just a little longer. Everything that follows will make better sense if you understand some of the principles behind an ultra training plan, and you need to do this before you lace up your shoes. It always helps to know why you should do something, and why you should do it in a particular way, before you set out on the journey of learning how to do it.

PLANNING – YOUR SECRET WEAPON

Imagine you're setting off on an overseas trip, and have just got off the plane in a city you have never been to before. You've heard about a divine local waterfall with hot springs at the bottom of it. It's hidden in thick jungle and difficult to get to, but you're determined to set out on the journey to find it. What's the first thing you do after you've got through immigration and had your passport stamped? Do you just start walking and hope to stumble across it? Unlikely. You're more likely to ask someone who has been there before to guide your journey. They'll be able to tell you about any obstacles to expect and the provisions you'll need along the way – maybe you'll need to camp out, maybe you'll need food. Your advisor might even be able to draw a map for you. With this help, you'll understand the journey ahead and what you need in terms of both your skill set and your knowledge. Sure, you can set off armed with nothing, and hope that you'll get lucky and stumble across the waterfall, but chances are it will take you a lot longer than if you'd first sought the guidance of someone who has been there before.

In this case, your divine waterfall is the finish chute of your first 100km ultramarathon. To get there, you're going to have to go on a journey. Not just a journey on race day, but a journey that starts with the preparation and planning necessary to ensure you are successful.

Having a plan in place is beneficial because it provides guidance and structure, helping to prevent you from becoming overwhelmed by the task at hand. Without a plan, you're leaving things up to chance. You can run out of time to refine and improve elements of your ultra running in your training, or even forget to work on whole elements. This leaves you feeling underprepared a few weeks out from your race, and that's certainly not the frame of mind you want to be in when you hit the start line.

Another benefit of having a specific plan in place is the focus, clarity and direction it brings to your training. As the saying goes, 'How do you eat an elephant? One bite at a time.' Ultra training is no different. The ultra plan allows you to focus on the one critical thing that you need to complete each and every day (unless, of course, it's a day off) in order for you to reach your ultra goal. This focus allows your mind to be at ease, as you know that over time all the required boxes of training and race preparation will be ticked. All you need to do is put your best effort into following the plan and what is prescribed in each session. Simple, right?

CONSISTENCY

No single training run, on its own, will deliver the improvements you're after. It is groups of training runs, blocks of training and long-term consistency that delivers results. A training plan is a vital component for ensuring that long-term consistency, and has a knack of ensuring your commitment. Often runners don't realise the importance or effect of a training plan until they have actually been on one. Once they *have* been on one, they're unlikely to go without one again. The run plan allows habits to be built and cemented into place. It enables you to start slowly and develop before progressing to the next step and building on your progress. These habits become routine and, before you know it, your fitness and skill level has shifted exponentially – and you have only just got started!

Beyond having a plan, great runners use a few others tricks to help them maintain long-term consistency. And while it sounds simple, one of these tricks is to keep a training diary. You have two options for this: pen and paper or an online program. Online options include programs such as Training Peaks (The Ultra Journey's go-to option), Strava (affectionately known as Facebook for athletes) or Garmin Connect, to name just a few. Whichever method you choose to use, the important thing is to keep some sort of diary. You will be amazed at the motivation it provides, as well as its ability to highlight where your training is consistent, and where it's not.

IT'S JUST 'PLAN A' – ADAPTABILITY

Another important principle you need to be aware of when it comes to your training plan is that it is exactly that: a plan. It's 'Plan A'. You need to be flexible with it. Without a plan you don't have anything to work from, but while the plan is essential, you also have to be prepared to be adaptable when required. Just as you will have to be adaptable in your ultra race. What are some of the things that will come up that require an adaptable plan? In a word: life ... work, travel, weather (especially hot days), unexpected fatigue, illness, family and kids, and on it goes.

This notion of adaptability applies not only to your planning, but to your running. By now you are well aware that we are discussing ultra running, which generally occurs on trails. Trails are a dynamic, ever-changing environment. They have steep uphills, they have technical downhills, they have loose footing, and there could even be scrambling. The environment cannot be as highly controlled as road running. This means that intensity levels can change and vary in nature, despite your best efforts to stick to your outlined training set. In ultra running, you need to adapt to this and look at the outcomes of the training set. Are you building your aerobic engine, your anaerobic ability, your run strength or maybe developing your knowledge around race nutrition? The outcome of the set could also be said to be its goal. If you focus on this goal, you'll be able to make the right adaptations when things don't go exactly to plan.

The training sets are designed to be completed on trails all around the world. But if your unique environment and circumstances require modification, then all we ask is that you complete the set to the best of your ability and try to achieve its particular focus or outcome. If at first you don't feel you are doing it 'right', don't worry. Continue to put in your best effort and you will make progress, you will continue to develop, and you will be smashing your training sets and ultra running goals in no time.

While we're on the subject of flexibility, I think it's time to bring up the subject of injuries. Your training is like a house of cards. You want it to be big, really big, but you have to be careful. If you injure yourself, it's like taking a card out – the whole structure comes crashing down. Result? Weeks or even months off running. A much better approach is to be slow, thorough and make sure your house is strong. Rarely do injuries 'just happen'; there are usually warning signs, or you bring them on by deciding to break the rules. If warning signs appear, it's better to slow down and take the necessary action to prevent the problem. A few days off training now and appropriate prevention (that's why that team is in place) is much better than forging ahead. You want to arrive at the start line with a big strong card tower, not one that's a heap of crumpled cardboard!

Illness must be treated in much the same way as injury, but is often unavoidable. Luckily, however, it generally lasts for a much shorter period. If illness strikes, you won't be able to continue with your original plan. Modifications will need to be made and new parameters put in place. You will need to take days off running to allow your body to repair and recoup. After this time training may be resumed, initially in a modified form, before a full training load can be resumed. Oh, and yes, you will be grumpy during this time – every runner is! But if you're this grumpy when you're ill, imagine how grumpy you will be if you dice with danger and bring the house of cards crashing down with no one to blame but yourself!

PERIODISATION – WORKING BACKWARDS FROM YOUR GOAL

Periodisation is a fancy name for the sequential, systematic and structured approach to your training program. In particular, it takes into account how the body adapts physiologically – that is, how your ultra runner body adapts to training – and creates a structure that works with and maximises this process. As part of this structure, periodisation includes times of loading and unloading the body, plus a taper (recovery and reduced run load prior to racing).

Understanding periodisation helps us to design an ultra running program that allows an individual to reach an optimal level of fitness for their goal race. While it can become quite involved for elite athletes, the basics of periodisation are easy to grasp, highly relevant and very useful for athletes who class themselves as beginner or intermediate runners chasing the ultra dream.

The five basics of periodisation are:

1. Weekly loading and recovery

2. Monthly loading and recovery

3. Structured approach to build up aerobic capacity

4. Structured approach to increase anaerobic threshold

5. Structured taper before the race.

To assist the runner in achieving their goals and to help periodisation be more effective, a segmented structure is used to build a training program. A complete program leading into a race or event is made up of blocks of training, and as you know, it's blocks of training that deliver results, not standalone run sets or one great week of running. Blocks of training are made up of weeks of training, which at the simplest level are made up of individual training sets. These individual training sets need to be scheduled in a way that allows them to be completed week on week. Applying all these concepts together forms the basis of periodisation.

The structure is sometimes given fancy names, such as microcycle, mesocycle and macrocycle, to give coaches a common language to use when discussing training plans. The time periods in each cycle (segment of training) can vary based on how you or a coach wants to structure the plan. Some elite athletes, who don't have to work and train as their main 'job', might use an eight-day or ten-day cycle. However, most ultra runners conform to a seven-day week to accommodate the demands of kids, work and a 'normal' life. Therefore, all plans detailed in this book work with a seven-day week as the short-term plan. This is then expanded to a four-week (one month) block, which is the medium-term plan. The long-term plan is the twenty-four week plan that leads up to race day.

Planning is all about beginning with the end in mind. When you plan something, anything, you have to start with your goal in mind and work backwards. What do you need to achieve in training to give you the confidence that you will have a great race? This becomes your end point and what you're aiming for in training. You then need to work gradually and systematically back from this point, week by week. Now, there are some obvious problems with this approach if you go it alone. You don't have the experience of having run 100km before, and possibly don't have years and years of endurance events or running under your belt. Conveniently, that's where this book and working with a coach or mentor comes in – to help fill in those blanks and provide insight into the things that you don't know, because often enough you don't even know just how much you don't know!

YOUR JOURNEY

With the previous point in mind, it can be a powerful exercise to write down where you think your end point needs to be. The two key questions to ask are:

1. What do you need to achieve in your final, peak week of training?

2. What else needs to have been covered in your training plan to give you confidence that you will have a great race?

After completing your list, take a moment to reflect on what has been covered so far. No doubt you have included many points in your list that would not have been there prior to reading this book. Assuming this is the case (shoot, we hope so) that is fantastic and helps to demonstrate how much progress you have already made!

        •• •• •• ••

Now you understand why it's so important to have a plan. Moreover, you know that your training plan is just that – a plan – and you're prepared to be flexible and adapt it where necessary. You understand the concept of periodisation and how you need to keep your eyes on the prize – your 100km ultra – and accept that your training will take a gradual, systematic approach that will build on itself week after week in the lead-up to your race. The next step is to dive into understanding the short, medium and long-term plans. You're almost there!

CHAPTER 12

BUILD AND ADAPT YOUR PLAN

At last, the moment you have been waiting for since Chapter 1 has arrived! This book is called *Journey to 100* for a reason. It's the journey towards your first 100km ultramarathon, and in this chapter we'll begin to map out the twenty-four week preparation that will see you through the race and crossing the finish line with all the glorious emotions that accompany such an achievement. We'll look at plans in the context of the short, medium and long term, learn what to expect from each phase, and understand how they fit together to create the six months of preparation you need leading up to your ultra. Most importantly, we'll also learn the art of adapting plans. It's important to have this knowledge so that you can take the detailed plans provided in the appendices of this book and tailor them to your specific needs.

SHORT-TERM PLAN (WEEK)

The short-term plan fits within a seven-day period. In other words, it's your weekly plan. Within the weekly plan, you need to understand how the various sets play off against one another. This helps to manage the run load. You don't want to have all your intense runs in a group, and you also need to be careful of the interplay between your long run(s) and your intense runs.

Further, you need to understand what an anchor set is, and how this forms the starting point for developing your weekly plan. An anchor set is a run set that must occur on a particular day. This could be for one of a number of reasons. For instance, you may run with a run group or running partner every Wednesday night at 6pm, and this set is always an interval set. This is not something that can be easily shifted, as you're unlikely to convince an entire run group to change nights just to accommodate you! As such, this particular set becomes an anchor set.

Many people find that their long run is one of their anchor sets. The long run often has to occur when you have more time available, such as on the weekend or a particular weekday when you don't work. As this is the most important set of the week and requires more time, it is also considered an anchor set.

Once you have determined one or two (and for some people three) anchor sets, you can plan the rest of the week's training around them. In doing that planning, a few training rules need to be observed:

1. Ideally you do not want two hard days of running in a row. Hard runs are your long run and intensity set(s).

2. You need balance across the week, so that all the running does not occur over only a few days. This sometimes happens when runners only run on Friday, Saturday and Sunday, or Saturday, Sunday and Monday.

3. Recovery needs to be taken into consideration after the long and intense runs. This is discussed later this chapter.

Here are some examples of how you could structure the plan:

OPTION 1: FRIDAY LONG RUN

Five runs per week

Something like this is often seen when kids are thrown into the mix!

M	T	W	T	F	S	S
Easy recovery run	Soul run	Intensity set	Day off	Long run	Recovery day	Intensity set

OPTION 2: SUNDAY LONG RUN, WITH THURSDAY INTENSITY SET COMPLETED WITH A RUN GROUP

Six runs per week

M	T	W	T	F	S	S
Recovery day	Intensity set	Recovery run	Intensity set with run group	Recovery run	Soul run	Long run

OPTION 3: MID-WEEK LONG RUN ON A DAY OFF FROM WORK

Four runs per week

M	T	W	T	F	S	S
Day off	No work – long run	Recovery day	Intensity set	Day off	Intensity set	Soul run

WHEN THE PROVERBIAL HITS THE FAN – HOW TO ADAPT YOUR PLAN

What we have discussed above is the ideal, but life will get in the way at some point and the best-laid plans will need to be modified or adapted. This could be for any one of a number of reasons: illness, unexpected work trips or issues with the kids, to name a few. As we discussed in the previous chapter, a plan is just that – a plan – and it needs to be adaptable.

If a set is missed the first option is to rearrange the plan. Sometimes a simple swap is all that's required, at other times you can add a 'make-up' run elsewhere in the week, and sometimes a session will need to be dropped altogether to ensure you're not putting yourself at risk of injury and over-training. When this happens, an understanding of how to restructure your week according to the training hierarchy, outlined below, is essential.

Training hierarchy:

1. Long Run

2. Intensity sets (one or two)

3. Soul run

4. Recovery run

If sessions need to be dropped, they should be dropped from the hierarchy from the bottom up. In other words, the first set that should be dropped is the recovery run. If another needs to dropped it should be the soul run and so on. Of course, the day or days that you need to take off to fulfil unexpected commitments may not nicely match up with your run plan. This means that the run week may need to be restructured slightly to allow the least important set to be dropped and the more important sets to remain.

Let's look at an example of a not-so-easy swap involving Option 3 that allows the runner to maintain their run program. Should the runner's day off shift to a Wednesday, their long run would also have to shift to a Wednesday. But this would mean attempting to complete their long run the day before a hard intensity set on the Thursday. It's likely that their long run would go well and they would be feeling great, as they've had an extra day of recovery. The intensity set, however, is likely to suffer, as they would still be fatigued from their long run. They may even manage to get through this set but get hit by fatigue the following weekend, when they find that the day off on Friday was not enough recovery time. A better option, if possible, would be to complete the long run on the Wednesday, complete intensity sets on the Friday and Sunday, and have Thursday as a day off. The run week would be rearranged to look as follows:

ORIGINAL RUN WEEK

M	T	W	T	F	S	S
Day off	No work – long run	Recovery day	Intensity set	Day off	Intensity set	Soul run

NEW RESTRUCTURED RUN WEEK

M	T	W	T	F	S	S
Day off	Day off	Long run	Recovery day	Intensity set	Soul run	Intensity set

It may not be possible to rearrange the plan like this, and this is simply one example of a range of possible new plans. Let's look at another one.

Running on a Friday may simply be impossible – the runner may have to drop kids at school in the morning and have an important work meeting that they know is going to run way past 5pm. And they know there's no way they're going to get their planned day off this week. Completing a long run through the week on a different day is simply out of the question. This would require a different approach. With Friday running not an option, we could look to complete the following:

ORIGINAL RUN WEEK

M	T	W	T	F	S	S
Day off	No work – long run	Recovery day	Intensity set	Day off	Intensity set	Soul run

NEW RESTRUCTURED RUN WEEK

M	T	W	T	F	S	S
Recovery day	Day off	Intensity set	Day off	Day off	Long run	Soul run

The benefit of this approach is that the runner manages to complete the long run for the week and still maintain one intensity set. Their second intensity set can't be retained, as the days available to run simply do not match with how runs could be planned. A mistake that many runners make is that they feel they should make up a set just because it is on their 'run plan'. But you can only do your best, so don't worry if you can't create the perfect schedule every week. Maintaining appropriate weekly run programming is the best option in this instance, as you don't want to adversely affect the following week of running or risk injury. Remember, it's about being as consistent as you can over the long term, not one perfect week.

MEDIUM-TERM PLAN – FOUR WEEKS (MONTH)

The next range of planning that you need to take into consideration is the medium-term or four-week plan. Conveniently, this is roughly equal to a month; however, for the sake of consistency month on month, it's best to work on a four-week block.

With the medium-term plan you need to be aware of loading and unloading the body. The full plan leading up to your race is developed off three weeks of building, followed by a recovery week. This allows a good balance for most ultra runners, with sufficient load being developed before a greater period of recovery is planned. It's important to note that a recovery week does not mean *no* running. During this week, we simply unload the body *relative* to the workload it has been completing.

This reduced loading is beneficial for a number of reasons.

- It helps to prevent injuries by giving the body a chance to recover.

- It allows a period of mental recovery through planned days off from running.

- It allows the runner to plan their maintenance sessions. This could be a monthly massage or visit to a health care provider – remember that team! This approach allows runners to be organised. You know when your recovery week will occur and can track forward. With this planning in place you are able to book your appointments in advance, knowing they will easily fit into your run schedule, and harmony reigns in the life of the ultra runner. ☺

- Long-term consistency is maintained – that golden rule!

- You hit the following week reinvigorated and roaring to get back into running again.

Once a regular running program has been established, you will find that taking one or two days off will make a huge difference. It's important to remember that the purpose of the recovery week is to recover, but you should expect some fatigue from running to remain. This is very different from a taper period, which is discussed in the next chapter. A word of caution: while you may not notice this fatigue, it will be present. Often runners don't notice it because they have become accustomed to it!

The aim of the recovery period is to reduce the training load, but at a minimum you need to retain the key long run. Depending on your weekly structure, this often means having a reduced load through the week. One or, if needed, two easy recovery runs replace the intensity sets during the week, but the weekend long run is retained. It's also important to have a few days completely free of running in this time, as outlined below.

Now let's look at how this works by taking Option 2 from earlier in this chapter – Sunday long run with intensity set on Thursday with a run group, and a total of six runs per week.

ORIGINAL RUN WEEK

M	T	W	T	F	S	S
Recovery day	Intensity set	Recovery run	Intensity set with run group	Recovery run	Soul run	Long run

IMPLEMENTATION OF A RECOVERY WEEK

M	T	W	T	F	S	S
Day off	Intensity set is changed to an easy recovery run	Day off	Intensity set with run group If needed this is also changed to an easy recovery run	Recovery run	Soul run	Long run

The above schedule allows the runner the flexibility to determine the length of recovery needed. Let's investigate this further. Monday and Wednesday are typically easier days. While Monday was originally a running-free day, Wednesday now is as well. However, by changing the first intensity run to an easy recovery run, which is also shorter, the runner is able to maintain the consistency of their program while decreasing the fatigue placed on the body. This is, in essence, giving the runner three days without a large run volume.

By the end of this time most runners will feel like they've had a sufficient break and be re-energised and ready to go again.

There is also a contingency plan in place should they feel like they need additional recovery. If this is the case, the Thursday intensity set can also be modified to an easy recovery run. And should it be needed, Friday can then be changed to a run-free day. This makes it possible for the runner to have up to five full days of recovery time, if required. However, it's important that they still run during this time, as five days without running can leave the body feeling lethargic. The benefit of this approach is that it has the runner ready to tackle their long weekend run – the most important set of the week, and generally the ultra runner's favourite.

LONG-TERM PLAN

The long-term plan is the focused training that you begin when you're working towards your goal race. Prior to the first twelve weeks of the ultra run program, it's best if you have been running regularly; it is not recommended that you start from scratch. If the gap between your current run volume and the first week of the 24-week program is too large, you risk injury: the chasm you are attempting to leap across is simply too wide. If you have not been running consistently, then you would need to complete a bridging run program to put regular running in place before starting the 24-week program.

One of the common misconceptions within the endurance running community is the belief that it is only what you do in the last twelve weeks leading into your race that counts. While the last twelve weeks may be pivotal, what can be achieved in that time depends on what a runner has put in place in the previous twelve weeks. And to extrapolate that further, what can be achieved in those twelve weeks is based upon your lifetime experience as a runner. Without a solid foundation in place, you cannot build the mansion that goes on top!

The long-term plan works with a twenty-four week block. The long-term plan is an important concept to understand, as it takes into account how the body responds to various training stimuli. As a result, this gives the plan distinct phases. These phases are sometimes given different names by different coaches, but the essence and objective of each phase is the same. These phases and their main objectives are:

BASE PHASE – build the aerobic base of the ultra runner

BUILD PHASE – incorporate more threshold and race pace efforts to greater simulate and prepare the body for race day

PEAKING PHASE – putting the icing on the cake

TAPER PHASE – allowing the body to recover from the fatigue it has experienced prior to event day (discussed at length in Chapter 13)

RACE OR EVENT DAY – the fun bit!

Structuring training in this manner has additional benefits for the ultra runner, in that it helps to break what is a considerable period of time into distinct and achievable chunks. This focuses your attention, and helps to decrease anxiety and the feeling that you're not going to be ready come race day. It also gives you the confidence that you're doing the right types of training at the right times.

When you then look at the 24-week program, you'll see that there are two distinct parts. During the first twelve weeks, you're ensuring that you will have the aerobic engine required to power you through the entirety of the coming race. In the final twelve weeks, with your 'engine' installed and working reliably, you can develop your ability to complete the distance at an improved pace. This is all relative to the individual and their personal pace, but the structure allows the program to be relevant for everyone from the slowest to the fastest runner.

Two key points to be aware with the long-term plan are that the phases are based upon how the body responds to training, and this affects the types of runs that you complete in each phase. Yes, the last twelve weeks are important, but you need a solid foundation upon which to build your mansion. Improving your endurance running ability is a slow process, but gains are available to anyone who is prepared to consistently and fully commit to the long-term plan.

Beyond the long-term plan you have the **ANNUAL PLAN**, and this takes into account a **RECOVERY AND TRANSITION PHASE**. This phase is needed for mental down-time and physical recovery from the race. Race recovery is investigated in Chapter 12 to provide some guidance on how to bring annihilated legs back to life.

RECOVERY

It is vital that the ultra runner understands that it's during recovery and rest that the body makes the adaptations to the exercise that has been performed. During running and exercise, you are breaking the muscles down. The muscles recover from this and repair themselves when you're at rest – this is when an improvement in your physical condition actually happens. This means that sufficient recovery time needs to be in place. Without it, you are simply loading up the body without giving it a chance to come back stronger.

Recovery takes various forms within the training plan and is all relative to the individual. For an experienced runner, a recovery day may involve completing a recovery run, while for someone who is newer to running a recovery day may be a day entirely free of running. And note that recovery needs to be included in the short-term plan as well as the medium-term plan. To recap the earlier discussion, in the short-term plan, recovery days need to be planned and the higher volume days need to be separated. In the medium-term plan, developing an easier week of running every three weeks is of great benefit to the ultra runner.

Recovery sessions are included in the training programs provided in the appendices of this book, and the recovery techniques you should use during these sessions are described below. If you have been prescribed exercise by a physiotherapist, these should also be undertaken during this time (and of course more frequently if they advise). Undertaking a short recovery session up to three times a week will go a long way to ensuring that you are fighting fit when you come to run.

Beyond the inclusion of days off or recovery days in the ultra program, there are additional techniques that can be incorporated. The aim of these techniques is to aid in recovery and to help ensure that injuries do not occur by keeping the body, especially the muscles, supple and able to perform their function.

The first and most important technique is one that runners find surprisingly hard to implement. Sleep! Ensuring that you get enough sleep is by far the best recovery method you have available; this is when the most repair occurs.

Additional to sleep, there are a range of manual manipulation techniques that can be used to enhance recovery. Two that need to be performed by a trained professional are remedial massage and dry needling. The need for a remedial massage therapist on your team has already been discussed; however, dry needling is also an excellent way to relieve tight, aching muscles. While remedial massage can be targeted, it's a shotgun approach when compared to the sniper-rifle approach of dry needling. This technique must be performed by a trained professional and is well worth consideration.

Beyond the professional services of remedial massage and dry needling, there are recovery techniques that the ultra runner can employ on their own. These include using a foam roller, massage ball, stretching and hitting the bath. As an ultra runner you're constantly beating yourself up on the trails, in your intensity sets and on your long run. You body needs some love! Ultra runners simply don't make time for these activities if they're not scheduled into the training program. The time taken does not need to be long and it should not be onerous, but it does need to happen.

Let's look at these DIY techniques in a bit more detail.

FOAM ROLLER – great for targeting the quads, calves and illiotibial band (ITB).

MASSAGE BALL – works best to dig into the glutes and hip flexors.

STRETCHING – this is an ongoing practice that must be undertaken regularly by the ultra runner. It is recommended that ultra runners target the following muscles:

- Calves
- Quads
- Glutes
- Hamstrings
- Hip flexors.

THE BATH – this is a great way to help relieve the muscles. It provides a fantastic way to ensure the muscles are warm prior to a stretching session. Some people choose to use Epsom salts, and while there is little evidence that they help, why not? Throw some bubbles in, turn a podcast on (The Ultra Journey Podcast is a great option … just saying!) and suddenly you have a great way to relax an ultra runner.

You have continued on your ultra journey and have built on your understanding of the key concepts of periodisation. You now understand how these affect the short, middle and long-term plan. You also understand that a plan is just that – a plan – and things won't always go to plan! (Dr. Seuss loved that one!) To that end, you understand how to restructure the training week if needed. You also

understand the importance of recovery and how this is structured within the program to ensure optimal outcomes for the ultra runner. But your understanding around recovery does not stop there; you have additional recovery techniques that may be used by the ultra runner, which is what the next chapter is all about. We did say this was an ultra journey!

CHAPTER 13

TAPERING

The taper is a period of prolonged recovery that allows the deep-set fatigue present in your body to disappear. A taper works because fatigue levels diminish at a faster rate than your fitness levels. This means that the fatigue you have become accustomed to running with disappears. While your fitness decreases slightly, it erodes at a much slower rate. This leaves you in fantastic shape to run your ultramarathon. Ultra runners who did not start their training plan early enough often overlook the need for this taper and decide to skip it. They feel that because their event is coming up, they must increase their running volume so they can feel confident about making the distance. They often decide to complete their longest run one weekend before their goal race. But this approach is fraught with danger. You can't cram for the ultra running test! The fatigue from completing your longest run this late in a training plan will not completely disappear by the following weekend. As a result, runners who make this mistake start their event on tired legs, rather than being fresh and raring to go.

The added benefit of a taper period is that it allows you to mentally prepare for your event. With your running time decreased, there is more time to spend on ensuring that your nutrition plan, pacing plan and gear are all properly organised. It's often the case that you have to travel to the event, which takes additional time, energy and organisation. Having this extra time available helps to relieve the stress of rushing about at the last minute.

So, you might be wondering when the taper period begins. Over time it has become apparent that a reduced week of running, followed by a two-week taper, works best. This means that your biggest run week will occur four weeks out from your event.

Now let's look at each component of the taper in more detail. These components are the reduced week, the taper two weeks out from your race (Taper 2) and the final race week preparations (Taper 1). Your goal 100km ultra will occur on the Saturday or, occasionally, the Sunday.

That means it looks like this:

- Biggest week
- Reduced week
- Taper 2
- Taper 1 – race week with 100km event on the Saturday or Sunday.

REDUCED WEEK

The reduced week is far from an easy week. It simply involves a reduction in the run volume that you have been tackling. In this week you reduce the volume, but keep one of the key intensity sets in place. The other intensity set is dropped to allow recovery after your biggest/peak run week. By this stage there is little to gain by either increasing run volume or maintaining a high volume. By contrast, you want to make sure that the running you're completing is all about quality with reference to your ultra race. This reduced week forms a midway point between your biggest week and the start of your official taper period.

The other important point to note is that this is the week when travel will need to occur if your event involves a significant time zone shift, or climate or altitude change. However, if the change is minimal, then travel can take place during either Taper 2 or Taper 1.

Following on from the example discussed in the previous chapter, the reduced week might look something like this:

M	T	W	T	F	S	S
Day off or walk 20–30 minutes	Day off	Easy recovery run following the big weekend runs	Soul run 80 minutes Stretching If needed this is also changed to an easy recovery run	Recovery techniques 20–30 minutes	Intensity set Visualisation session	Reduced long run While reduced, quality running is included Stretching

TAPER 2 – TWO WEEKS TILL RACE DAY

This is when the taper really starts and race mode kicks in. The last big set for ultra runners occurs in this period, ideally no closer than ten days out from the event. If you wish to complete a fitness test or time trial, this is the week when it should be done. While you will not be completely recovered when you undertake the fitness test, your fatigue will have diminished enough to allow an accurate test.

We're pretty certain your race will go well, but if you do make a goof ball of your race, the fitness test is a handy measure to reflect on. A fitness test is also useful if you want to compare your fitness across different races. Remember that ultra races are highly variable in their nature, weather conditions, course (ascents and descents) and altitude. The fitness test gives you a standard measure so that you can compare your fitness leading into different ultras. Yes, we have an inkling you'll be back for more, so we're setting you up for long-term success should you wish to see your progress year on year.

While a fitness test can be great, as discussed in Chapter 4, you need to proceed with caution. The focus at this point in the training plan is on having a great event, and completing a fitness test comes a very distant second. There'll be a lot going on at this time that can stress you out, and if leaving out the fitness test will help you relax, then go ahead and leave it out. If you find you're attaching a lot of emotion and anxiety to the test – if you feel like you're walking into an exam – just skip it. For others, 'life' will turn on extra stressors – illness, family issues, work problems – and adding a fitness test to the mix will be an extra stress that you'd rather be without.

You may also find that you're unduly upset over a perceived poor result. If you do have a negative result, you need to frame it as just a small part of a bigger picture. However, if for *any* reason you think the fitness test could have a negative impact on the race, it should be dropped in favour of a standard intensity set or, if needed, additional recovery. In an ideal situation a fitness test will fit perfectly, but we are human beings, not robots. Keep your eye on the prize!

Ten to fourteen days out from race day there is little to gain from prolonged hard training. While the longer runs have already decreased in volume, at this point the intensity sets are also decreased. Your focus shifts to making sure your body is mentally and physically feeling great for the day. The running you do at this point is all about making sure your body is still ticking over. In this period you want to remind the energy systems, muscles – and your mind – that you have a job at hand. The plan is designed to provide just a little bit of stimulation, almost teasing the body. This prevents the body becoming lethargic and helps to settle the mind for the impending event. Some runners love taper time, but most ultra runners hate it. They always feel they should be doing more and question their training. But because you have a structured ultra training plan in place and have been following a process, you don't need to worry about this. All your hard work is done, and you are about to reap the benefits!

VISUALISATION

The time freed up by the reduction in running can be put to great use. This is the week that you ensure your mindset is in place. More than half the job has been done; you have tackled a training program that focuses on key ultra running areas and tackled numerous challenges to develop your ability. Yet we have one more trick up our sleeve to help create the right mindset. This is the point at which visualisation sessions are built into the ultra running program. Let's look at visualisation in more detail.

Visualisation works because your mind does not realise that what you visualise is yet to occur; your mind thinks it has already happened. This means that if you picture yourself overcoming challenges, you will know what to do when those same challenges get thrown at you in reality. Similarly, if you visualise having a perfect ultra race, your mind will think that this has happened! And if you follow the program of planned visualisation, you're going to have your perfect ultra race not once or twice, but eight times before you hit the start line!

There are three steps to the visualisation process:

1. See yourself having a perfect race.

2. See yourself encountering all the obstacles, challenges and concerns that you're worried about. However, as each obstacle presents itself, visualise yourself overcoming it and having a great race. In your imagination, work your way through a race that has every single imaginable problem, each of which fails to stop you. You recover and start running strongly again. You finish your dream ultra and succeed!

3. Now complete your ultra again. This time visualise yourself having a fantastic race where everything goes perfectly. This is what you finish your visualisation session with – your perfect race.

The visualisation session should take place at a time and place when you can be fully relaxed and won't be interrupted. Some people prefer to lie on their bed, others sit or lie on the couch, and some tackle their visualisation in the bath! The key is to be stress free, thus allowing your mind to vividly see your perfect race unfold. In total it's only going to take about twenty minutes for you to relax and work through each of the scenarios, but that's time well invested.

To intensify your visualisation, try to attach positive emotion to your race as it unfolds. For most people, what they see and feel, both physically and emotionally, provides the deepest experience. What do you smell? Enrich the experience; take a deep breath of the clean mountain air. What do you see? Turn the colour up, make it rich and vibrant! What do you hear? Is it the sound of quiet footsteps or excited anticipation in the air? How does your body feel physically? You are strong, tenacious and capable. And most importantly, how does your body feel emotionally? Embrace the infectious energy that engulfs you! You can have your perfect race in your mind, and doing so will enable you to have your perfect race come graduation day.

Again, following the example already discussed, Taper 2 would look something like this.

M	T	W	T	F	S	S
Day off	Fitness test or last intensity set	Day off – walk as needed	Easy recovery run Visualisation session	Day off	Reduced soul run Visualisation session	Reduced long run

TAPER 1 – RACE WEEK

The last week before your big day follows a similar pattern to Taper 2. The volume and training stimulus drops further, with a few dabbles in intensity to keep the body awake and feeling fresh, and to ensure that lethargy doesn't set in. But while the training has dropped further, there are plenty of other tasks on the ultra runner's mind.

Any necessary travel generally occurs at the start of this week, unless there is a large time zone, altitude or climate change to manage. Naturally, the closer to home the race is, the later in the week the travel can safely take place. But keep in mind that check-in and race briefings often occur on the Thursday and Friday before the event, and you can't miss these.

Everyone's travel requirements will be different, and this affects each plan individually. Often running is dropped on the day or days of travel and substituted for a short walk upon arrival to help loosen the legs.

Let's look at an example that assumes that travel occurs on the Monday. This means the week looks as follows:

M	T	W	T	F	S	S
Travel followed by a short 20-minute walk	Easy Zone 1/ Zone 2 run & stretching. Massage if needed (recommended) but the massage must occur after the run	Easy run with short intensity segments. Visualisation session	Easy Zone 1/ Zone 2 run. Stretching. Carbohydrate-rich meal for dinner	Day off if you can cope or very easy 20-minute run. Event check-in and race briefing. CHO loading. Optional visualisation session	Race day – the ultra graduation	Party time & recovery time

You're nearly there, but there is one final topic to discuss. This is the all-important topic of fuelling your body prior to race day. Of course, I'm talking about the concept of carbohydrate, or CHO loading, as discussed in Chapter 5.

CHO LOADING

While having a bulletproof nutrition plan for race day is important, you need to start thinking about nutrition a few days before that. You are going to expect something extra special of yourself on race day, which means you want to hit the start line with a full fuel tank. If you don't, you're going to have to ask more of your body while you run, which simply doesn't make sense. What does make sense is making it as easy on your body as possible. That's where CHO loading comes in. This is about ensuring your fuel sources are full to the brim, but you're not bloated. When you CHO load, you're ensuring that the glycogen stores in both your muscles and your liver are full – really full.

In a way similar to tracking and planning your CHO for your race, you need to calculate what you need to eat in the twenty-four hours before the race. Some people CHO load for a full forty-eight or seventy-two hours prior to the event, but I believe this is a little excessive as it can leave you feeling flat. The approach I'm going to outline is one that is completed during the twenty-four hours prior to race start, along with ensuring a CHO-rich meal the night before commencing the loading period.

Let's investigate this a little further. Two nights before the event, I recommend having a CHO-rich meal. This can be made up of pasta, rice, potato or your choice of another CHO-rich option. The main thing to ensure is that you have a normal meal for yourself, but one that has a significant component of CHO. Are you having a Caesar salad? No, it has to have a significant CHO source.

Part of the reason why just having a normal meal works is because you're tapering. This reduced workload means that your body is not requiring as much CHO as it did during the height of your training. The added benefit of this approach is that it allows you to relax up until the final morning prior to the race. When you wake the next morning, twenty-four hours prior to the race, the CHO loading starts and your approaching event gets real, very real! This action will change your mindset as you shift from training and taper mode to full race mode. Delaying this mindset shift as long as possible is a really positive thing to do – you won't benefit from increasing your stress levels earlier than this point.

So how much CHO should you be putting into your system during this period? Suzanne Girard Eberle, the author of *Endurance Sports Nutrition*, recommends that athletes carbohydrate-load in the range of 8–10g per kg per day for males, while females need to be slightly higher at 12g per kg per day.[21] For your final twenty-four hours, the day before race day, we need to use the following formula to calculate your recommended CHO intake.

WEIGHT IN KG X 10 = CHO CONSUMPTION

If we apply this formula to a 65kg male, we get: 65 x 10 = 650g. This means that a 65kg male would be aiming to consume 650g of CHO over the entire day.

It may not sound like a lot, but if you don't do it correctly you will

21   Suzanne Girard Eberle, MS, RDN, CSSD, Endurance Sports Nutrition – Fuel your body for optimal performance, 3rd edn, Human Kinetics, 2014

be eating an entire Christmas dinner party for one! The result? You rock up at the start line feeling like a baby elephant, which is clearly not ideal. So let's look at the tricks that experienced runners use.

Follow a CHO-rich diet for the day, following your usual eating pattern. Let's assume this is breakfast, snack, lunch, snack, dinner. You then need a few additional items; the ones that give you a huge CHO bang for your buck. With your morning snack, have a sports drink; with lunch, power through 600ml of Coke or similar, and with your afternoon snack or dinner, have another 600ml sports drink. In short you drink your carbohydrate. If, after you have calculated your CHO for the day and you think that you're going to be falling a little short, throw in a couple of lollies (candy) over the day, or have some supper before bed (fruit salad is a great option).

This format should have you easily meeting your CHO-loading needs. We also recommend that, the first few times you CHO load, you record what you eat to get a reference on your consumption. After undertaking the above procedure a few times, you will learn what's required to meet your needs, and this approach becomes a stress-free way to achieve your desired outcome.

A word of warning: notice that all the foods mentioned above were low in fibre and 'food bulk'. This is no accident. While you only CHO load for the final twenty-four hours, you want to be limiting your fibre intake for twenty-four to forty-eight hours before the race. Failure to do so can leave you shooting for the bathroom as the jostling effect of running, well, runs its course! Yes, I am aware that you normally eat the brown bread, the brown rice, the brown pasta, adore celery and have a triple kale smoothie with muesli for breakfast, but now is not the time!

In short, the essentials are: drink your carbohydrate, limit your fibre and aim to consume your body weight in kg x 10g-worth of CHO in the twenty-four hours prior to your run.

Yee-haw! Suddenly you're one step closer! You now understand the taper period, including a reduced week, Taper 2 and Taper 1 – Race week. You understand that during this time run volume is decreased, but initially intensity remains. You understand where in the taper to implement a fitness test, but recognise that the objectives of this fall a distant second to the ultimate goal: a good race day. Further to this, you understand that approximately ten days out is a key marker for the turning point in the program, as running beyond this point does not increase your fitness on race day. Your mindset is going to be on-point because you're going to employ visualisation over the final two weeks of your ultra plan. You are going to have your perfect race because you have seen it happen before!

CHAPTER 14

ULTRA RACE DAY AND BEYOND

All that's left to do now to get you started on your journey is to lock in a race day, then turn to the end of the book and find the plan that works best with your schedule. But before you do that, I want to pass on all my tips on how to have a fantastic race day – the final hurdle. While you have all the knowledge, fitness and experience required to front up at the start line knowing that you will make it to the finish, it's certainly not going to be easy. It's going to challenge you. If this weren't the case, then everyone would be doing it and there would be little satisfaction in your goal. But you're about to put yourself among a select few who can say, 'I have run a 100km ultra-marathon.' You will soon be able to wear that title with pride and have a bright shiny buckle to prove it! You will have an experience you never forget, with stories to last a lifetime. You are coming to the conclusion of your journey and will reach the pinnacle as you run the last emotion-packed 100m to the finish line. Imagine that feeling, a feeling of euphoria that no one can ever take away from you and only someone who has been there can relate to.

The final points that need to be covered to ensure your confidence come race day are: nutrition planning, special needs bags, aid stations, helpers/pacers and the inevitable race morning nerves. Experience suggests that you're going to tackle more than one ultra … scary thought … and so we also look at a post-race recovery plan and race evaluation.

NUTRITION

It is recommended that you start undertaking your nutrition plan early in the race, while you still feel 'good'. By frontloading your nutrition, you can then ease back in the later stages of the race when you start to feel like you've been chewed up and spat out! This might mean that over the first half of the ultra, you consume CHO at 10–15g per hour more than you do over the back part of the race. For example, you might start consuming it at 75g per hour, and drop this back to 65g per hour beyond the six-hour mark.

The nutrition choices we make early in the race are also different from what they are later. Ultra races generally start early in the morning, and consuming sports gels at 7:30am can be a bit much to handle. It makes more sense to start on the savoury foods; for example, have a wrap early in the race, then proceed to a formulated sports drink such as Tailwind or Infinit (two brands popular with ultra runners) after a few hours. Later in the race, we may need to incorporate some savoury foods again if flavour fatigue (getting sick of only having sweet foods or one type of food) becomes an issue. This approach of having a range of foods and slightly decreasing your CHO intake gives you the best chance of minimising possible nutrition problems.

Now let's revisit the nutrition planning introduced in Chapter 5, and build race preparation into the process.

1. Work out the number of hours that you anticipate you will run for.

2. Work out the amount of CHO you would like to consume per hour (50–90g).

3. Lay out your nutrition for each hour in a separate pile. Be aware of what you intend to take from aid stations, and take this into account with your calculations.

4. Place nutrition in drop bags, if applicable, to ensure you don't have to carry all your nutrition.

DROP BAG PREPARATION

Thought needs to be put into your drop bags over the final few weeks of your training plan. Be mindful that some races require you to drop off your bags the day before the race, while some only require you to drop them off on race morning. This can affect the type of foods you can use – perishable foods may not be suitable. Ideally you should sort out your drop bags a few days before the event, then, if needed, finalise them just prior to dropping them off.

What goes into the bags will vary for everyone, but there are two broad categories that need to be catered for: nutrition and comfort. Bag drops can also be used to decrease the weight of the items you have to carry. You can leave some items in appropriate bags for collection or use later. Items that fall into this category include, but are not limited to:

- Nutrition items
- Sunscreen
- Anti-chafe cream (Body Glide)
- Warm clothes, e.g. a fleece that is not part of your mandatory gear.

When planning your drop bags, it can be helpful to play the 'What if?' game. What if I get a blister? What if my shoes are wet? What if it takes me longer than I anticipated? What if? You need to be sure that you can continue on to the following checkpoint and finish line using only what is on your person or in your drop bags, so plan them accordingly, but do be careful not to over-complicate things. While you may not need to stop and collect a drop bag at each aid station, the first part of your planning should always consider your required nutrition.

It is also recommended that at one checkpoint, around the 70–75km mark if possible, you have a more substantial drop bag containing:

- Small towel or face washer, to wash and dry feet as needed
- Small bottle of water (to enable the above)
- Spare shoes and socks
- Blister pads or similar.

Optional items that may be needed at particular stages of the race include:

- Spare head torch or spare batteries.
- Small bottle of sunscreen.
- Run shoes if you're coming out of a section of course that's likely to make your feet wet, but precedes a section that is likely to be dry. For example, a section that takes place along a beach before heading inland.
- Spare run top, shorts and underwear.
- Warm base layer, top and pants. This is particularly useful when

anticipating a finish time after dark, as the final hours can be cold and you don't want to have sweaty gear on that makes you even colder. It's important to note that as your pace will be lower than your training runs, you will not generate as much heat as you normally do. Anticipate this in your planning.

You need to clearly mark your bag for easy identification when coming into the collection point. Inexperienced runners often overlook the importance of this. However, if you consider the number of entrants in the field, you can quickly assess how many bags are likely to be at each drop point. You might consider writing on the bag in a distinctive-colour permanent marker, as well as tying a brightly coloured ribbon to it. While some races have volunteers who will help locate your bag, expect to have to do this yourself.

After your bags are all organised and marked, make sure to drop them at the appropriate location before the race. You don't want your bag drops in the wrong order.

NEGOTIATING AID STATIONS AND BAG DROPS

Whether you're racing or not, you want to be fast through aid stations and your bag drop, and you should approach them in a similar way. Smooth is fast. But this certainly does not mean that you are rushing. To put things in perspective, let's say you take an extra six minutes per aid station because you were tardy. Over five aid stations, that adds another thirty minutes to your finish time. Just as importantly, we want you to remain focused on your end goal and be quick through the aid stations and bag drops, as this helps you to maintain a positive mindset. So let's look at how you go about achieving a smooth, speedy experience.

As you are coming into an aid station or bag drop, you need to think about and mentally prepare what you're going to do. This requires some on-course visualisation. Know the tasks you must complete and their likely order. They might look something like this:

1. Fill up water bladder and flasks.

2. Collect drop bag.

3. Replace nutrition in run-pack.

4. Collect head torch.

5. Attend to hot spot(s) to prevent them from developing into a blister.

6. Pack items not required back into drop bag.

7. Keep running.

If you're coming through an on-course aid station and you don't have a drop bag waiting for you, the list of tasks will be much simpler. Depending on your nutrition plan, it may look something like this:

1. Empty snap-lock bag of pre-measured nutrition supplement into bladder.

2. Refill bladder and bottles with water.

3. Collect on-course nutrition. (Make sure you know exactly what you need, i.e. 1 x gel, 1 x sports bar, etc., but be equally prepared to be flexible if these are not available, which means knowing your approximate CHO values.)

Now a word about water. Water is heavy. You want to determine before each aid station approximately how much you need for the following segment of the race. Your aim is to carry enough so that you don't run out, but not so much that you carry excess between stations. This is all planned pre-race and modified as you progress, depending on how you're going.

For example, there may be 10km between the start line and check-point one, and 20km between checkpoint one and checkpoint two. Based on having the same water requirement between each, you have to take twice the water on at checkpoint two. There is no advantage in carrying excess water for the first portion of the race when you can simply fill up at checkpoint one. Carrying your entire fluid requirement from the start to the second checkpoint would mean taking enough for 30km. While you could achieve this, a short stop and refilling at the first checkpoint decreases the weight you have to carry at the start line and is the way to go.

HELPERS AND PACERS

Some races allow you to have helpers or pacers. The job of a helper is to make your journey through aid stations quicker. They are able to hand over your pre-planned nutrition, have run gear available, and allow you to have a range of options available at each checkpoint. It also enables you to have the luxury of asking for particular equipment to be available further up the track. For instance, a rain jacket if you notice you're starting to get cold, or new shoes if you decide you would benefit from them.

While helpers can be great, they need to have easy access to your run gear, and understand what gear they will be passing to you at each station. To help helpers in their job, it's recommended that you still separate your expected requirements at each aid station into different bags. And while helpers can make transitions at aid stations quicker, it is important not to get caught talking and sitting around. As discussed above, taking too long at aid stations adds significant time to your overall result. Keep focused on the task at hand.

Pacers perform a different function; while they can help you at an aid station, they're also able to run sections of the course with you. Generally, pacers can't start the race with you, but can join you from a designated checkpoint. Normally a pacer (or run buddy) is able to run with you from about half way or more into the race. It's important that the pacer knows their role – their main aim is to ensure your safety. Beyond this, they can make your time on the trail more fun and interesting because it becomes a shared experience. But they must be up to the task! While your pace will be slower than your typical pace, you don't want to end up being the one who is supporting the supporter! Make sure a pacer has the experience to run the required distance, over the required terrain, and at a suitable pace.

A pacer's tasks can be defined by the following objective: forcing you to make positive decisions late in the race. After all, by this stage you might not be thinking quite as clearly as at the start of the race. Just saying! A knowledgeable pacer can influence and assist you in the following areas:

- Pacing – obvious, right?
- Nutrition

- Mindset – a.k.a. encouragement
- Comfort – for instance, checking you're warm enough.

THE START LINE AND HOW TO GET THERE ON TIME

Race day is now here. Don't expect to have a great sleep the night before. You will be nervous. If you have slept well, great, but if you haven't you're among the majority. Don't be concerned by this, as it's unlikely to affect your race day. It's the sleep that you get over the few days prior that matters.

When you wake up, food is again on the cards, despite having eaten plenty the day before. You need to top up that fuel tank. For breakfast the morning before the race, we need to consider foods that are in keeping with our CHO loading. They want to be low in fibre, high in CHO and easy to digest. Many will choose to steer clear of significant amounts of milk at this point, but this is really a personal preference. The alternative to milk is a couple of slices of white toast with honey, jam or vegemite. However, if you can tolerate milk, a low-fibre cereal will certainly do the trick. You may choose to have tea or coffee with this. This can be especially handy, as the caffeine can have the desirable effect of stimulating nervous bowels. A nervous, pre-race poop in the comfort of your own accommodation is much more desirable than waiting in a long portaloo line at race start. We did say that we were going to leave no stone unturned!

After eating I recommend going for a short walk. Just for ten to fifteen minutes. This has a twofold effect: it helps your legs to wake up after sleeping and gives you time to focus on the task at hand.

Runners are used to running kilometre upon kilometre on their own, and this is likely to be the only solitude you enjoy for the day. At the start line there will be people everywhere, many wanting your time. People will be wishing you well and there will be training partners that you will talk to. You also have a warm-up to complete and possibly bags to check in.

There will also be plenty of 'noise' leading into the race. You will hear it all around you; people will question you. What do I mean by this? The noise you are going to hear is whether you're prepared. People will question you on your training. How long was your longest run? How many hills did you run? What's your nutrition plan? What's your pacing plan?

There are two main reasons people ask these questions. While they may not realise it, they're trying to get you to doubt your training, question yourself and question your self-belief. If they create this self-doubt in you, it makes them feel better. Why? Because they're not ready. They doubt their own training, their own preparation, their own lead-up. If they create doubt in you and your training, it makes them feel better.

So what do you do? Don't listen; ignore it and quiet your mind. You have done the training and have followed a specific ultra running plan, you have given yourself an ultra education; you are ready. Trust in your training, trust in the process you have been through, trust in what you have done and, above all, believe in yourself.

The last point we need to cover here is the start itself. Take it in. Remember it. You have worked hard for this moment and it's one of the best feelings in the world. Look around, feel the energy, remember your journey and how far you have come. Pinch yourself. You want this moment, this experience, burned into your memory. You only get to stand at the start line of your first 100km ultra once. It is truly amazing. Then wait and listen for the familiar horn or cannon that will send you on your way. After this, all that's left to do is enjoy the journey.

POST-RACE RECOVERY PLAN

While all you're going to want to do the day after you race is lie on the couch or sit in the coffee shop and swap stories, it's really important that you keep active. However, under no circumstances is a run suggested!

Being active means walking … lots of walking. This should be short and slow at first, but build in duration. You will also find that your walking pace will naturally pick up as life is breathed back into your legs. Guidance on how long to walk for and a suitable walk progression is provided in the recovery plan below. At this point, it's also worth revising the recovery options available to the ultra runner.

In the first few days after your ultra, you're likely to be too sore to undertake the manual manipulation techniques discussed earlier, but after about four days these techniques can be employed. During the second week after your event, you should continue regular walking and stretching and using the foam roller and massage ball, and also book in for a second massage. If you get the urge to run again, try to ignore it until at least ten days after your event and then build into it slowly. Complete short runs of twenty and thirty minutes before attempting anything longer. Equally, don't be scared to extend this no-running period out to a full two weeks if you feel you need it.

14-DAYS POST-RACE RECOVERY PLAN

Day 1	Day 2	Day 3	Day 4	Day 5	Day 6	Day 7
Walk 20 minutes Light stretching	Walk 20 minutes	Walk 30 minutes Light stretching	Walk 30 minutes Massage	Walk 40 minutes Foam roller and massage ball can now be used	Day off	Walk 40 minutes Light stretching

Day 8	Day 9	Day 10	Day 11	Day 12	Day 13	Day 14
Walk 40 minutes Complete post-race evaluation (discussed below)	Day off	Walk 30 minutes Foam roller & massage ball	Very easy 20-minute run Massage	Day off	Very easy 30-minute run	Very easy 40-minute run

RACE EVALUATION

Regardless of whether or not you plan to complete another 100km ultra, a post-race evaluation can provide insight. It is, however, not recommended that you complete this immediately after your run. You're likely to be highly emotional during this time. It's much better to allow everything about the experience to sink in and review your race and training about a week later. Raw emotion will have passed, but the race will be recent enough to allow clarity.

It's important that you review both your race and your training. Regardless of whether you're happy or disappointed about the outcome of the race, take time to reflect on the entire journey. Especially look back on how far you have come – it is with this perspective that athletes gain clarity. They begin to fully appreciate what they have achieved in their running, and how far their self-belief has come. More often than not this correlates with amazing personal development in their life outside of running. This is something you should be proud of!

When undertaking an evaluation, there is no need to make it difficult or long-winded. The aim is to use the experience to its full potential to allow maximum personal growth.

The following questions provide a useful guide to direct your thinking.

1. Race details: you may include weather, overall time, age-group place, overall place

2. Brief recap of the day

3. Strengths

4. Focus areas for improvement

5. Interesting/other points.

Areas to consider for strengths and areas for improvement include your training leading up to the race, and the race day itself. It's recommended that you take the time to fill in the evaluation form below. The items in the evaluation form are in no way exhaustive, nor will everything apply to you; they're simply to provide some guidance.

The first part is an overall evaluation using the questions from the above list, which is followed by a more focused evaluation that allows you to consider some areas that may have been overlooked.

Overall evaluation	
Race	
Guiding question	Notes
Race details • Weather • Overall time • Age-group place • Overall place	
Brief race day recap	
Strengths	
Focus areas for improvement	
Interesting or additional points	

Focused evaluation		
Guiding area	Race day	Training prior
Game plan • Longest run prior (time & distance) • Biggest run week prior (time & distance) • Consistency achieved in training • Nutrition plan • Pacing plan • Fitness test (including best result achieved)		

Focused evaluation		
Guiding area	Race day	Training prior
Game plan (cont.) • Recovery • Taper • Race simulation • Gear selection		
Body • Aerobic development • Anaerobic development • Run strength • Stretching • Recovery practices • Massage • Physiotherapist or similar • Injuries		
Techniques • Uphill • Downhill • Cadence & efficiency • Pacing (implementation) • Nutrition (implementation)		
Mindset • Belief in self • Attitude • Flow • Visualisation • Peak sensation		

Ready, set, go! You now have all the underpinning knowledge required to be successful in your ultra journey. Race day will be a breeze! Sure, there will be nerves and sure, it's going to challenge you, but trust in your training and yourself. You have now covered the final components needed. Bag drop: check. Aid stations: check. Helpers and pacers: check. Finish line: check. Start line, 'Yep, I'm going to remember that one!' But as this is unlikely to be your last ultra, you're going to be keen to get back to running soon. Come on … one ultra simply won't be enough! You're going to be keen to continue your journey, continue the fun and improve further.

'And will you succeed? Yes, you will indeed, 98¾% guaranteed! Kid you'll move mountains!'[22]

---

22   Dr Seuss, *Oh, the places you'll go!*, Random House, 1990

CONCLUSION

You have now completed your ultra journey! Go you! As you reflect on the journey, you might realise that you have already improved as a runner.

At this point we'd like you to take the quiz again, and compare your new score to your old score to see just how far you've come. The improvement in your score has come about because you have implemented the lessons, taken action and commenced one of the ultra training plans to build on your ultra running experience. All that's left is for you to attend your own ultra running graduation ceremony – your first 100km ultramarathon!

And after that? First of all, celebrate what you have achieved, then begin looking forward once again. If you were fortunate enough to complete your first 100km ultra close to home, you can now look interstate and overseas for your next big adventure, as destination races abound. Or you might look to run faster over the distance and set a PB or PR. If you're looking for a different challenge, there are many other events that ultramarathoners set their sights on. For example, going beyond the 100km mark or working towards 100 miles. But don't limit your sights there; multi-stage running races probably don't seem so daunting now. The options are aplenty. But it's not just about running. Many ultra runners say that ultra running is a metaphor for life. They want to know what else they're capable of, what else they can achieve. Their self-improvement in ultra running goes hand in hand with their self-improvement in life. Ultra running is their way of life.

This book was not written simply to be read. This book was written to give you confidence and self-belief in your ultra running. It was written to get you out there running, to allow you to dream big and achieve your impossible! For those who are willing to share their journey with my community at The Ultra Journey, I say thank you. And I also have a request: The Ultra Journey would love you to share your journey. Take photos along the way, especially at your graduation ceremony, so that we can share your happiness. You can post your photos here:

Facebook: https://www.facebook.com/theultrajourney
Instagram: theultrajourney #theultrajourney

Journey to 100 started with a sad story, but finishes with a very different one…

Sarah coasted along the trail, checking her watch; 79km was the number she saw illuminated. Checkpoint five was about 3km ahead; she was past the magic 70km mark and exceeding all her expectations. It was late afternoon and she was running well. She had started with confidence and that confidence had never left her.

She reflected back to the start of her training, and asked herself: 'Why am I doing this? To prove to myself I can, and to show my kids that if they set their mind to a challenge, they can achieve it.' The journey had challenged and changed her and she had grown from it. She had grown both personally and in her understanding of ultra training. A grin rolled over her face; she now had an ultra running education and was about to pass her graduation test.

As the track started to climb she sailed effortlessly up the hill. Her pacing was flawless. She ran the usual checklist over her body.

Hydration: check, going well. Nutrition: check; her nutrition plan was on song. She was feeling great and running strongly. As the emotion of the event swept over her, the grin on her face was replaced by a broad smile as a tear ran down her face. She almost couldn't believe what she was about to achieve. The finish line was now becoming a reality. As she ran along she could see it in her mind. The cheers, the lights, the finish arch, a chair and a bright shiny buckle. But more importantly, the smiles on her husband's and kids' faces. It was all within reach. This first chapter of her ultra running was coming to a close and boy, had she enjoyed the journey. With a smile still on her face, on she ran…

But this is your story, not Sarah's. You still need to write the final page. If you have entered your first 100km ultra, well done. And if you entered this race while you were reading this book, we're super proud of you. If you are yet to enter a 100km ultra, this is your number one priority. Put this book down and go and do it now! What are you waiting for? It's time to make your dream a reality! The time is now…

Enjoy the ultra journey!

GUIDE TO THE TRAINING PROGRAMS

Ensuring everything is in place prior to your goal race is a mammoth task. I've covered a lot of elements in this book – but how are you going to practise and refine them all into your training? With a plan, of course! The following programs are all about a plan of action. A detailed plan that is developed to cater for your ultra runner goals. A plan that also takes into account your many obligations in life and at work to create the balance you need for a long-term commitment to your training. This allows you to be a successful ultra runner.

After reading this book, you have all the underpinning knowledge and understand the principles required to complete your ultra run plan. All runners will come with different anchor sets, different prior experience and different lead-up races planned. The plans presented here will accommodate the most common training needs. If the plans don't quite match your unique needs, then you're encouraged to identify the patterns, structure and processes that are used in these ultra plans and have been discussed throughout this book. Using the plans and your new-found ultra education as a guide, you will need to make adjustments to the plan that is the closest fit to your individual needs. I know you can do it!

HOW TO READ THE TRAINING PROGRAMS

The three training programs are set out in table format, so that you can take in the information at a glance. However, this means that a lot of abbreviations and symbols are used. They might even look like gobbledygook the first time you try to follow them. After a while, however, reading them will be a breeze. To that end, we've provided the following instructions, plus a glossary of the terms the tables contain.

The following instructions on how to read the training sets refer to the first set on the first Tuesday of the first 24-week program in Appendix 1. So just find that set, and read through the following 'translation'. Everything will soon be crystal clear.

EASY, MEDIUM, HARD
- The title of the set.

Total time: 60 minutes
- The approximate time taken to run the set.

WARM-UP
- The instructions under this heading form your warm-up.

10 minutes Z1 building to Z2
- The first part of the warm-up is ten minutes running spent building from Zone 1 to Zone 2.

2 x 3 minutes building over the 3 minutes to Z4
- The second part of the warm-up comprises two three-minute running efforts. In each effort you build over the

three minutes from a Zone 2 intensity at the start, to a Zone 4 intensity at the end.

4 minutes Z2 running

- This indicates four minutes of Zone 2 running to finish the warm-up and allow you to prepare for the main part of the set, which comes next.

MAIN SET

- The instructions under this heading form your main set.

2 (3 x 5 minutes)

- The main set is made up of two sets, indicated by the figure 2 at the front of the brackets. Each set comprises three repetitions, each five minutes in duration, which is indicated by the figure 3 x 5 inside the brackets.

1. 5 minutes easy

- Signifies that the first (1) of the three reps is five minutes easy.

2. 5 minutes medium

- Signifies that the second (2) of the three reps is five minutes medium.

3. 5 minutes hard

- Signifies that the third (3) of the three reps is five minutes hard.

Repeat for a total of two sets

- Reminds you that you need to complete the above for a total of two sets.

COOL DOWN

- The instructions under this heading form your cool down.

10 minutes easy Z1 running

- Just like it says, you should do ten minutes of Zone 1 running.

Walk & stretch as needed

- A friendly reminder to walk and stretch if you have time.

GLOSSARY OF TERMS

EFFORTS – the component of running when you're running or working harder (the bit that requires more effort).

HR – heart rate.

REPS – repetitions; the number of efforts you will complete.

RI – rest interval; the recovery period between the efforts. Sometimes the rest interval is a complete rest, but normally it's a jogging recovery.

STRIDES – relaxed, faster-paced running. Not so hard that you're labouring, but you're moving freely and enjoying the increased pace.

WARNING

If the running volume in the first week of these plans is greater than 10% of your current volume, then a bridging program is recommended. Additionally, note that it is not ideal to transfer straight from a road running program to a pure trail and ultra running program. This adjustment should be made over a period of time to reduce the chance of injury. Additionally, if you are concerned about injury from running at higher paces, the following plans will need to be modified and those higher paced efforts changed to efforts at a lower intensity level.

24 WEEKS TO 100KM, LONG RUN ON SUNDAY

This program is ideal for somebody who works Monday to Friday.

WEEK 1: 24 WEEKS TO RACE DAY – BASE PHASE 1

Monday	Tuesday	Wednesday	Thursday	Friday	Saturday	Sunday
Day off	**Easy, medium, hard**	**Walk**	**4/3/2/1 fartlek set**	**Recovery day**	**Soul run – trail**	**Long run – trail**
It is recommended that you look through the first week of training and refer to the intensity guide to ensure you're ready to hit the ground running!	Total time: 60 minutes	20–30 minutes	Total time: 60 minutes		1 hour 30 minutes	2 hours 20 minutes
	Warm-up		*Warm-up*		Aim to gradually build into your running over the first 10 minutes	*Warm-up*
	10 minutes Z1 building to Z2		10 minutes Z1 building to Z2			10 minutes Z1
	2 x 3 minutes building over the 3 minutes from Z2 to Z4		4 x 1-minute strides on a 1-minute easy jogging recovery			10 minutes building to Z2
	4 minutes Z2		2 minutes Z2			*Main set*
	Main set		*Main set*			Aim to hold a Z1/Z2 effort –where possible target Z2
	2 (3 x 5 minutes)		This main set is all about starting to learn your zones and how to vary your pace to match each. As you shift to a higher zone you should be running just a little harder.			Include walk breaks when necessary. A couple of minutes every 20–60 minutes is recommended.
	1. 5 minutes easy					*Cool down*
	2. 5 minutes medium		4 minutes Z2			10 minutes easy Z1 running
	3. 5 minutes hard		3 minutes Z3			
	Repeat for a total of two sets		2 minutes Z4			
	Cool down		1 minute Z5b			
	10 minutes easy Z1 running		Repeat the main set x 3			
	Walk & stretch as needed		*Cool down*			
			10 minutes easy Z1 running			
			Walk & stretch as needed			

WEEK 2: 23 WEEKS TO RACE DAY – BASE PHASE 1

Monday	Tuesday	Wednesday	Thursday	Friday	Saturday	Sunday
Recovery day	Descending pyramid	Walk	Fitness test No 1 – 30-minute time trial	Recovery techniques	Soul run – trail	Long run – trail
	Total time: 62 minutes	20–30 minutes	Total time: 70 minutes	20–30 minutes	1 hour 30 minutes	2 hours 30 minutes
	Warm-up		Refer to Chapter 4	Refer to Chapter 12	Aim to gradually build into your running over the first 10 minutes.	*Warm-up*
	10 minutes Z1 building to Z2					10 minutes Z1
	2 x 3 minutes building over the 3 minutes from Z2 to Z4					10 minutes building to Z2
	4 minutes Z2 running					*Main set*
	Main set					Aim to hold a Z1/Z2 effort - where possible target Z2
	This set is a pyramid, where the recovery is half the time of the work interval. Aim to complete the recovery component at Z2 intensity.					Include walk breaks when necessary. A couple of minutes every 20–60 minutes is recommended.
	6 minutes Z3, 3 minutes Z2					*Cool down*
	5 minutes Z4, 2.5 minutes Z2					10 minutes easy Z1 running
	4 minutes Z4, 2 minutes Z2					
	3 minutes Z5a, 90 seconds Z2					
	2 minutes Z5b, 60 seconds Z2					
	1 minute Z5b, 30 seconds Z2					
	Cool down					
	10 minutes easy Z1 running					
	Walk & stretch as needed					

WEEK 3: 22 WEEKS TO RACE DAY – BASE PHASE 1

Monday	Tuesday	Wednesday	Thursday	Friday	Saturday	Sunday
Recovery day	**Four squared**	**Easy recovery run**	**Fitness test No 2 – 60-minute aerobic threshold test**	**Recovery techniques**	**Soul run – trail**	**Long run – trail**
	Total time: 61 minutes	20 minutes Z2	Total time: 90 minutes	20–30 minutes	1 hour 30 minutes	2 hours 40 minutes
	Warm-up	Spend the first 10 minutes building to Z2	Refer to Chapter 4	Refer to Chapter 12	Aim to gradually build into your running over the first 10 minutes	*Warm-up*
	10 minutes Z1 building to Z2					10 minutes Z1
	2 x 3 minutes building over the 3 minutes from Z2 to Z4					10 minutes building to Z2
	4 minutes Z2 running					*Main set*
	15 minutes Z2 running					Aim to hold a Z1/Z2 effort –where possible target Z2
	Main set					Include walk breaks when necessary. A couple of minutes every 20–60 minutes is recommended.
	4 x 4 minutes					*Cool down*
	Each 4-minute block is broken into 1/2/1: the first minute is Z1/2, the next two minutes are Z4 and the final minute is Z5b					10 minutes easy Z1 running
	Cool down					
	10 minutes easy Z1 running					
	Walk & stretch as needed					

WEEK 4: 21 WEEKS TO RACE DAY – BASE PHASE 1 (RECOVERY WEEK)

Monday	Tuesday	Wednesday	Thursday	Friday	Saturday	Sunday
Recovery day	**Easy strides**	**Day off**	**Fitness test No 3 – uphill time trial**	**Recovery techniques**	**Soul run – trail**	**Long run – trail**
Schedule a remedial massage if possible	Total time: 50 minutes		Refer to Chapter 4	20–30 minutes	1 hour 40 minutes	2 hours 50 minutes
	Warm-up		*If an additional day of rest is required, shift this set to Saturday and remove the Saturday soul run. Instead, complete an easy 30 minute Z2 recovery run.*	Refer to Chapter 12	Aim to gradually build into your running over the first 10 minutes	*Warm-up*
	10 minutes Z1					10 minutes Z1
	10 minutes Z2					10 minutes building to Z2
	Main set					*Main set*
	10 x 1-minute strides:					Aim to hold a Z1/Z2 effort – where possible target Z2
	Complete 10 x 1 strides at Z3 on a 1-minute Z2 recovery.					
	Try to run according to feel and keep the strides comfortable and easy					Include walk breaks when necessary. A couple of minutes every 20–60 minutes is recommended.
	Cool down					
	10 minutes easy Z1 running					Include one 30-minute segment of Z3 running. Aim to complete this segment on a prolonged uphill if possible.
	Walk & stretch as needed					
	If you feel more recovery is required change this set to a 30-minute Z2 recovery run					*Cool down*
						10 minutes easy Z1 running

231

WEEK 5: 20 WEEKS TO RACE DAY – BASE PHASE 2

Monday	Tuesday	Wednesday	Thursday	Friday	Saturday	Sunday
Day off	**12-minute ramps** Total time: 69 minutes *Warm-up* 10 minutes Z1 building to Z2 2 x 3 minutes building over the 3 minutes from Z2 to Z4 *Main set* 3 x 12 minute builds: 3 minutes Z2 3 minutes Z3 3 minutes Z4 3 minutes Z5b At the conclusion of each block include a 1-minute walk. *Cool down* 10 minutes easy Z1 running Walk & stretch as needed	**Easy recovery run** 30 minutes Z2 Spend the first 10 minutes building to Z2	**4/3/2/1 max intensity builds** Total time: 60 minutes *Warm-up* 10 minutes Z1 building to Z2 4 x 1-minute strides on a 1-minute easy jogging recovery 12 minutes Z2 *Main set* Take the first 30 seconds to build into each of the efforts. 4 minutes Z5b 4 minute Z2 3 minutes Z5b 3 minute Z2 2 minutes Z5b 2 minute Z2 1 minute Z5b 1 minute Z2 *Cool down* 10 minutes easy Z1 running Walk & stretch as needed	**Recovery techniques** 20–30 minutes Refer to Chapter 12	**Soul run – trail** 1 hour 50 minutes Aim to gradually build into your running over the first 10 minutes	**Long run – trail** 3 hours *Warm-up* 10 minutes Z1 10 minutes building to Z2 *Main set* Aim to hold a Z1/Z2 effort – where possible target Z2 Include walk breaks when necessary. A couple of minutes every 20–60 minutes is recommended. *Cool down* 10 minutes easy Z1 running

WEEK 6: 19 WEEKS TO RACE DAY – BASE PHASE 2

Monday	Tuesday	Wednesday	Thursday	Friday	Saturday	Sunday
Day off	**Pyramid fartlek**	**Easy recovery run**	**Hard/easy**	**Recovery techniques**	**Soul run – trail**	**Long run – trail**
	Total time: 67 minutes	30 minutes Z2	Total time: 60 minutes	20–30 minutes	2 hours	3 hours 10 minutes
	Warm-up	Spend the first 10 minutes building to Z2	Warm-up	Refer to Chapter 12	Aim to gradually build into your running over the first 10 minutes	Warm-up
	10 minutes Z1 building to Z2		10 minutes Z1 building to Z2			10 minutes Z1
	2 x 3 minutes building over the 3 minutes from Z2 to Z4		4 x 1-minute strides on a 1-minute easy jogging recovery			10 minutes building to Z2
	Main set		2 minutes Z2			Main set
	Complete the following pyramid alternating between Z2 and Z4:		Main set			Aim to hold a Z1/Z2 effort – where possible target Z2
	4 minutes Z4		15 x 1 minutes on a 1-minute Z2 recovery:			Include walk breaks when necessary. A couple of minutes every 20–60 minutes is recommended.
	5 minutes Z2		1–8 at Z4			
	6 minutes Z4		9–15 at Z5a			
	7 minutes Z2		Cool down			Cool down
	6 minutes Z4		10 minutes easy Z1 running			10 minutes easy Z1 running
	5 minutes Z2		Walk & stretch as needed			
	4 minutes Z4		Be aware that HR will not respond completely during the efforts so you will have to rely on your feel for your output or RPE			
	Cool down					
	10 minutes easy Z1 running					
	Walk & stretch as needed					

WEEK 7: 18 WEEKS TO RACE DAY – BASE PHASE 2

Monday	Tuesday	Wednesday	Thursday	Friday	Saturday	Sunday
Day off	**12-minute ramps**	**Easy recovery run**	**Pyramid down**	**Recovery techniques**	**Soul run – trail**	**Long run – trail**
	Total time: 82 minutes	30 minutes	Total time: approx. 60 minutes	20–30 minutes	2 hours 10 minutes	3 hours 20 minutes
	Warm-up	Z2	*Warm-up*	Refer to Chapter 12	Aim to gradually build into your running over the first 10 minutes	*Warm-up*
	10 minutes Z1 building to Z2	Spend the first 10 minutes build-ing to Z2	10 minutes Z1 building to Z2			10 minutes Z1
	2 x 3 minutes building over the 3 minutes from Z2 to Z4		4 x 1-minute strides on a 1-minute easy jogging recovery			10 minutes building to Z2
	Main set		2 minutes Z2			*Main set*
	4 x 12 minute builds:		*Main set*			Aim to hold a Z1/Z2 effort – where possible target Z2
	3 minutes Z2		Run straight through:			Include walk breaks when necessary. A couple of minutes every 20–60 minutes is recommended.
	3 minutes Z3		6 minutes Z2 1 minute Z5b			
	3 minutes Z4		5 minutes Z2 1 minute Z5b			
	3 minutes Z5b		4 minutes Z2 1 minute Z5b			Include one 20-minute segment of Zone 3 running. Aim to complete this segment on a prolonged uphill if possible.
	At the conclusion of each block include a 1-minute walk		3 minutes Z2 1 minute Z5b			
			2 minutes Z2 1 minute Z5b			*Cool down*
	Cool down		1 minutes Z2 1 minute Z5b			10 minutes easy Z1 running
	10 minutes easy Z1 running		*Cool down*			
	Walk & stretch as needed		10 minutes easy Z1 running			
			Walk & stretch as needed			

WEEK 8: 17 WEEKS TO RACE DAY – BASE PHASE 2 (RECOVERY WEEK)

Monday	Tuesday	Wednesday	Thursday	Friday	Saturday	Sunday
Day off	6-squared run	Day off	Hill reps 6 x 3 minutes	Recovery techniques	Soul run – trail	Long run – trail
Schedule a remedial massage if possible	Total time: 66 minutes		Total time: approx. 75 minutes	20–30 minutes	2 hour 20 minutes	3 hours 30 minutes
	Warm-up		Warm-up	Refer to Chapter 12	Aim to gradually build into your running over the first 10 minutes	Warm-up
	10 minutes Z1 building to Z2		10 minutes Z1 building to Z2			10 minutes Z1
	2 x 3 minutes building over the 3 minutes from Z2 to Z4		4 x 1-minute strides on a 1-minute easy jogging recovery			10 minutes building to Z2
	Main set		2 minutes Z2			Main set
	6 x 6 minutes:		Main set			Aim to hold a Z1/Z2 effort – where possible target Z2
	3 minutes Z2		6 x 3-minute hill reps building to Z5b on an easy Z1 descent and 60 seconds Rl			Include walk breaks when necessary. A couple of minutes every 20–60 minutes is recommended.
	2 minutes Z3		This means that you run the hill or part of a hill from a chosen start point for 3 minutes duration. At this point hit the lap button on your watch. Turn for an easy recovery jog down the hill.			Include one 30-minute segment of Zone 3 running. Aim to complete this segment on a prolonged uphill if possible.
	1 minute Z4		Upon reaching your start point have a 60-second rest and then repeat. Complete this for a total of 6 reps.			Cool down
	Cool down		Cool down			10 minutes easy Z1 running
	10 minutes easy Z1 running		10 minutes easy Z1 running			
	Walk & stretch as needed		Walk & stretch as needed			
	*If you feel more recovery is required, change this set to a 30-minute Z2 recovery run.					

WEEK 9: 16 WEEKS TO RACE DAY – BASE PHASE 3

Monday	Tuesday	Wednesday	Thursday	Friday	Saturday	Sunday
Day off	**Uphill effort – 15 minutes** Total time: 80 minutes *Warm-up* 10 minutes Z1 building to Z2 2 x 3 minutes building over the 3 minutes from Z2 to Z4 10 minutes Z2 *Main set* 1 x 15 minutes uphill effort Z4 After completing the effort continue to the top of the hill or to an appropriate point that will allow an approx. 80-minute run. Following the effort continue at a Z2 intensity. On the descent target a Z2 intensity where possible; however, be aware that you will likely also spend considerable time in Z1 and this is fine. *Cool down* 10 minutes easy Z1 running Walk & stretch as needed	**Easy recovery run** 20 minutes Z2 Spend the first 10 minutes building to Z2	**Hill reps 7 x 3 minutes** Total time: approx. 80 minutes *Warm-up* 10 minutes Z1 building to Z2 4 x 1-minute strides on a 1-minute easy jogging recovery 2 minutes Z2 *Main set* 7 x 3-minute hill reps building to Z5b on an easy Z1 descent and 60 seconds RI. This means that you run the hill or part of a hill from a chosen start point for 3 minutes duration. At this point hit the lap button on your watch. Turn for an easy recovery jog down the hill. Upon reaching your start point have a 60-second rest and then repeat. Complete this for a total of 7 reps. *Cool down* 10 minutes easy Z1 running Walk & stretch as needed	**Recovery techniques** 20–30 minutes Refer to Chapter 12	**Soul run – trail** 2 hours 30 minutes Aim to gradually build into your running over the first 10 minutes	**Long run – trail** 3 hours 40 minutes *Warm-up* 10 minutes Z1 10 minutes building to Z2 *Main set* Aim to hold a Z1/Z2 effort – where possible target Z2 Include walk breaks when necessary. A couple of minutes every 20–60 minutes is recommended. *Cool down* 10 minutes easy Z1 running

WEEK 10: 15 WEEKS TO RACE DAY – BASE PHASE 3

Monday	Tuesday	Wednesday	Thursday	Friday	Saturday	Sunday
Day off	**Uphill Effort – 20 minutes**	**Easy recovery run**	**Hill reps 5 x 5 minutes**	**Recovery techniques**	**Soul run – trail**	**Long run – trail**
	Total time: 80 minutes	35 minutes Z2	Total time: approx. 80 minutes	20–30 minutes	2 hours 40 minutes	3 hours 50 minutes
	Warm-up	Spend the first 10 minutes build-ing to Z2	*Warm-up*	Refer to Chapter 12	Aim to gradually build into your running over the first 10 minutes	*Warm-up*
	10 minutes Z1 building to Z2		10 minutes Z1 building to Z2			10 minutes Z1
	2 x 3 minutes building over the 3 minutes from Z2 to Z4		4 x 1minute strides on a 1-minute easy jogging recovery			10 minutes building to Z2
	10 minutes Z2		2 minutes Z2			*Main set*
	Main set		*Main set*			Aim to hold a Z1/Z2 effort – where possible target Z2
	1 x 20 minutes uphill effort Z4		5 x 5-minute hill reps building to Z5a on an easy Z1 descent and 60 seconds RI			Include walk breaks when necessary. A couple of minutes every 20–60 minutes is recom-mended.
	After completing the effort, continue to the top of the hill or to an appropriate point that will allow an approx. 80-minute run. Following the effort continue at a Z2 intensity.		*Cool down*			*Cool down*
			10 minutes easy Z1 running			10 minutes easy Z1 running
	On the descent target a Z2 intensity where possible; however, be aware that you will likely also spend considerable time in Z1 and this is fine		Walk & stretch as needed			
	Cool down					
	10 minutes easy Z1 running					
	Walk & stretch as needed					

WEEK 11: 14 WEEKS TO RACE DAY – BASE PHASE 3

Monday	Tuesday	Wednesday	Thursday	Friday	Saturday	Sunday
Day off	Uphill effort – 3 x 10 minutes	Easy recovery run	Hill reps 6 x 5 minutes	Recovery techniques	Soul run – trail	Long run – trail
	Total time: 80–90 minutes	30 minutes Z2	Total time: approx. 80 minutes	20–30 minutes	2 hours 50 minutes	4 hours
	Warm-up	Spend the first 10 minutes building to Z2	Warm-up	Refer to Chapter 12	Aim to gradually build into your running over the first 10 minutes	Warm-up
	10 minutes Z1 building to Z2		10 minutes Z1 building to Z2			10 minutes Z1
	2 x 3 minutes building over the 3 minutes from Z2 to Z4		4 x 1-minute strides on a 1-minute easy jogging recovery			10 minutes building to Z2
	Main set		2 minutes Z2			Main set
	3 x 10 minutes uphill effort:		Main set			Aim to hold a Z1/Z2 effort - where possible target Z2
	1 x 10 minutes Z3		6 x 5-minute hill reps Z4 on an easy Z1 descent			Include walk –breaks when necessary. A couple of minutes every 20–60 minutes is recommended.
	2 x 10 minutes Z4		Cool down			Cool down
	All on a 4-minute Z2 recovery		10 minutes easy Z1 running			10 minutes easy Z1 running
	After completing the effort, continue to the top of the hill or to an appropriate point that will allow an approx. 80-minute run. Following the effort continue at a Z2 intensity.		Walk & stretch as needed			
	On the descent target a Z2 intensity where possible; however, be aware that you will likely also spend considerable time in Z1 and this is fine					
	Cool down					
	10 minutes easy Z1 running					
	Walk & stretch as needed					

WEEK 12: 13 WEEKS TO RACE DAY – BASE PHASE 3

Monday	Tuesday	Wednesday	Thursday	Friday	Saturday	Sunday
Day off	**Easy recovery run**	**Day off**	**4/3/2/1 max intensity builds**	**Recovery techniques**	**Soul run – trail**	**Long run – trail**
Schedule a remedial massage if possible	Total time: 60 minutes		Total time: 60 minutes	20–30 minutes	3 hours	4 hours 15 minutes
	Warm-up		*Warm-up*	Refer to Chapter 12	Aim to gradually build into your running over the first 10 minutes	*Warm-up*
	10 minutes Z1		10 minutes Z1 building to Z2			10 minutes Z1
	10 minutes building to Z2		4 × 1-minute strides on a 1-minute easy jogging recovery			10 minutes building to Z2
	Easy 30-minute Z2 run.		2 minutes Z2			*Main set*
	This can be completed on the trails or road.		*Main set*			Aim to hold a Z1/Z2 effort – where possible target Z2
	Cool down		Take the first 30 seconds to build into each of the efforts.			Include walk breaks when necessary. A couple of minutes every 20–60 minutes is recommended.
	10 minutes easy Z1		4 minutes Z5b 4 minute Z2			
			3 minutes Z5b 3 minute Z2			Include one 30-minute segment of Zone 3 running. Aim to complete this segment on a prolonged uphill if possible.
			2 minutes Z5b 2 minute Z2			
			1 minute Z5b 1 minute Z2			
			Cool down			*Cool down*
			10 minutes easy Z1 running			10 minutes easy Z1 running
			Walk & stretch as needed			

PROGRAM ONE

WEEK 13: 12 WEEKS TO RACE DAY – BUILD PHASE 1

Monday	Tuesday	Wednesday	Thursday	Friday	Saturday	Sunday
Day off	**Uphill eff ort – 3 x 10 minutes**	**Easy recovery run**	**Hill reps 6 x 5 minutes**	**Recovery techniques**	**Soul run – trail**	**Long run – trail**
	Total time: 80–90 minutes	30 minutes	Total time: approx. 80 minutes	20–30 minutes	2 hours 50 minutes	4 hours 30 minutes
	Warm-up	*Spend the first 10 minutes building to Z2*	*Warm-up*	Refer to Chapter 12	Aim to gradually build into your running over the first 10 minutes	*Warm-up*
	10 minutes Z1 building to Z2		10 minutes Z1 building to Z2			10 minutes Z1
	2 x 3 minutes building over the 3 minutes from Z2 to Z4		4 x 1-minute strides on a 1-minute easy jogging recovery			10 minutes building to Z2
	Main set		2 minutes Z2			*Main set*
	3 x 10 minutes uphill effort:		*Main set*			Aim to hold a Z1/Z2 effort – where possible target Z2
	1 x 10 minutes Z3		6 x 5-minute hill reps Z4 on a 4-minute easy Z1 descent			Include walk breaks when necessary. A couple of minutes every 20–60 minutes is recommended.
	2 x 10 minutes Z4		This means that you will not quite return to your start point during this time and so will gradually make it further and further up the hill.			*Cool down*
	All on a 4-minute Z2 recovery		*Cool down*			10 minutes easy Z1 running
	After completing the effort, continue to the top of the hill or to an appropriate point that will allow an approx. 80-minute run. Following the effort continue at a Z2 intensity.		10 minutes easy Z1 running			
	On the descent target a Z2 intensity where possible, however, be aware that you will likely also spend considerable time in Z1 and this is fine		Walk & stretch as needed			
	Cool down					
	10 minutes easy Z1 running					
	Walk & stretch as needed					

240

WEEK 14: 11 WEEKS TO RACE DAY – BUILD PHASE 1

Monday	Tuesday	Wednesday	Thursday	Friday	Saturday	Sunday
Day off	Uphill effort – 15/10/5 minutes	Easy recovery run	Hill reps 3 x 8/4 minutes	Recovery techniques	Soul run – trail	Long run – trail
	Total time: 80–90 minutes	35 minutes Z2	Total time: approx. 80 minutes	20–30 minutes	2 hours 50 minutes	4 hours 45 minutes
	Warm-up	Spend the first 10 minutes building to Z2	*Warm-up*	Refer to Chapter 12	Aim to gradually build into your running over the first 10 minutes	*Warm-up*
	10 minutes Z1 building to Z2		10 minutes Z1 building to Z2			10 minutes Z1
	2 x 3 minutes building over the 3 minutes from Z2 to Z4		4 x 1-minute strides on a 1-minute easy jogging recovery			10 minutes building to Z2
	Main set		2 minutes Z2			*Main set*
	1 x 15 minutes Z3		*Main set*			Aim to hold a Z1/Z2 effort – where possible target Z2
	1 x 10 minutes Z4		3 x 12 minutes as 8 minutes Z3 into 4 minutes Z4 on a 4-minute easy Z1 descent. Turn and repeat.			Include walk breaks when necessary. A couple of minutes every 20–60 minutes is recommended.
	1 x 5 minutes Z4					
	All on a 4-minute Z2 recovery		This means that you will not quite return to your start point during this time and so will gradually make it further and further up the hill.			*Cool down*
	After completing the effort, continue to the top of the hill or to an appropriate point that will allow an approx. 80-minute run. Following the effort continue at a Z2 intensity.		*Cool down*			10 minutes easy Z1 running
			10 minutes easy Z1 running			
	On the descent target a Z2 intensity where possible; however, be aware that you will likely also spend considerable time in Z1 and this is fine		Walk & stretch as needed			
	Cool down					
	10 minutes easy Z1 running					
	Walk & stretch as needed					

WEEK 15: 10 WEEKS TO RACE DAY – BUILD PHASE 1

Monday	Tuesday	Wednesday	Thursday	Friday	Saturday	Sunday
Day off	**Uphill effort – 15/10/5 minutes**	**Easy Recovery Run**	**Hill reps 3 x 8/4 minutes**	**Recovery techniques**	**Soul run – trail**	**Long run – trail**
	Total time: 80–90 minutes	40 minutes	Total time: approx. 80 minutes	20–30 minutes	3 hours	5 hours
	Warm-up	Spend the first 10 minutes building to Z2.	*Warm-up*	Refer to Chapter 12	Aim to gradually build into your running over the first 10 minutes	*Warm-up*
	10 minutes Z1 building to Z2		10 minutes Z1 building to Z2			10 minutes Z1
	2 x 3 minutes building over the 3 minutes from Z2 to Z4		4 x 1-minute strides on a 1-minute easy jogging recovery			10 minutes building to Z2
	Main set		2 minutes Z2			*Main set*
	15/10/5 minutes uphill effort as follows:		*Main set*			Aim to hold a Z1/Z2 effort – where possible target Z2
	15 minutes Z4 on a 6-minute Z2 recovery		3 x 12 minutes as 8 minutes Z3 into 4 minutes Z4 on a 4-minute easy Z1 descent. Turn and repeat.			Include walk breaks when necessary. A couple of minutes every 20–60 minutes is recommended.
	10 minutes Z4 on a 4-minute Z2 recovery					
	5 minutes Z4 followed by a 2-minute walk for a job well done		This means that you will not quite return to your start point during this time and so will gradually make it further and further up the hill			*Cool down*
	After completing the effort, continue to the top of the hill or to an appropriate point that will allow an approx. 80-minute run. Following the effort continue at a Z2 intensity.					10 minutes easy Z1 running
	On the descent target a Z2 intensity where possible; however, be aware that you will likely also spend considerable time in Z1 and this is fine		*Cool down*			
			10 minutes easy Z1 running			
	Hint: it is recommended that you start at the lower end of Z4 for the first 15-minute block. You can then increase the intensity towards the upper end of Z4 over the 10 and 5-minute period if needed.		Walk & stretch as needed			
	Cool down					
	10 minutes easy Z1 running					
	Walk & stretch as needed					

WEEK 16: 9 WEEKS TO RACE DAY – BUILD PHASE 2 – RECOVERY WEEK

Monday	Tuesday	Wednesday	Thursday	Friday	Saturday	Sunday
Day off	Easy strides	Day off	Hill reps 6 x 6 minutes	Recovery techniques	Soul run – trail	Long run – trail
Schedule a remedial massage if possible	Total time: 50 minutes		Total time: approx. 80 minutes	20–30 minutes	3 hours	5 hours 15 minutes
	Warm-up		Warm-up	Refer to Chapter 12	Aim to gradually build into your running over the first 10 minutes	Warm-up
	10 minutes Z1		10 minutes Z1 building to Z2			10 minutes Z1
	10 minutes Z2					10 minutes building to Z2
	Main set		4 x 1-minute strides on a 1-minute easy jogging recovery			*Main set*
	10 x 1-minute strides					Aim to hold a Z1/Z2 effort – where possible target Z2
	Complete 10 x 1-minute strides Z3 on a 1-minute Z2 recovery. Try to run on feel and keep the strides comfortable and easy.		2 minutes Z2			Include walk breaks when necessary. A couple of minutes every 20–60 minutes is recommended.
			Main set			
			6 x 6-minute hill reps:			*Cool down*
	Cool down		1 & 2 at Z3			10 minutes easy Z1 running
	10 minutes easy Z1 running		3–6 at Z4			
	Walk & stretch as needed		All on a 4-minute easy Z1 descent			
	If you're feeling more recovery is required, change this set to a 30-minute Z2 recovery run.		This means that you will not quite return to your start point during this time and so will gradually make it further and further up the hill			
			Cool down			
			10 minutes easy Z1 running			
			Walk & stretch as needed			

WEEK 17: 8 WEEKS TO RACE DAY – BUILD PHASE 2

Monday	Tuesday	Wednesday	Thursday	Friday	Saturday	Sunday
Day off	**Split the hill**	**Easy recovery run**	**Hill reps 7 x 6 minutes**	**Recovery techniques**	**Soul run – trail**	**Long run – trail**
	Total time: 80–90 minutes	40 minutes Z2	Total time: approx. 90 minutes	20–30 minutes	3 hours	5 hours 30 minutes
	Warm-up	Spend the first 10-minutes building to Z2	*Warm-up*	Refer to Chapter 12	Aim to gradually build into your running over the first 10 minutes	*Warm-up*
	10 minutes Z1 building to Z2		10 minutes Z1 building to Z2			10 minutes Z1
	2 x 3 minutes building over the 3 minutes from Z2 to Z4		4 x 1-minute strides on a 1-minute easy jogging recovery			10 minutes building to Z2
	Main set		2 minutes Z2			*Main set*
	2 x 15-minute uphill efforts:		*Main set*			Aim to hold a Z1/Z2 effort – where possible target Z2
	1 x 15-minute Z4 on a 6-minute Z2 recovery		7 x 6-minute hill reps:			Include walk breaks when necessary. A couple of minutes every 20–60 minutes is recommended.
	1 x 15-minute Z4		1 & 2 at Z3			*Cool down*
	After completing the effort, continue to the top of the hill or to an appropriate point that will allow an approx. 80-minute run. Following the effort continue at a Z2 intensity.		3–7 at Z4			10 minutes easy Z1 running
	On the descent target a Z2 intensity where possible; however, be aware that you will likely also spend considerable time in Z1 and this is fine		All on a 4-minute easy Z1 descent			
	Hint: it is recommended that you start at the lower end of Z4 for the first 15-minute block. You can then increase the intensity towards the upper end of Z4 over the 10 and 5-minute period if needed.		This means that you will not quite return to your start point during this time and so will gradually make it further and further up the hill			
	Cool down		*Cool down*			
	10 minutes easy Z1 running		10 minutes easy Z1 running			
	Walk & stretch as needed		Walk & stretch as needed			

WEEK 18: 7 WEEKS TO RACE DAY – BUILD PHASE 2

Monday	Tuesday	Wednesday	Thursday	Friday	Saturday	Sunday
Day off	**Split the hill 2 x 15 minutes**	**Easy Recovery Run**	**Hill reps 7 x 6 minutes**	**Recovery techniques**	**Soul run – trail**	**Long run – trail**
	Total time: 80 minutes	40 minutes Z2	Total time: approx. 90 minutes	20–30 minutes	4 hours	4 hours
	Warm-up	Spend the first 10 minutes building to Z2.	Warm-up	Refer to Chapter 12	Aim to gradually build into your running over the first 10 minutes	Warm-up
	10 minutes Z1 building to Z2		10 minutes Z1 building to Z2			10 minutes Z1
	2 x 3 minutes building over the 3 minutes from Z2 to Z4		4 x 1-minute strides on a 1-minute easy jogging recovery			10 minutes building to Z2
	Main set		2 minutes Z2			Main set
	2 x 15-minute uphill efforts:		Main set			Aim to hold a Z1/Z2 effort – where possible target Z2
	15 minutes Z4 on a 5-minute Z2 recovery		7 x 6-minute hill reps:			Include walk breaks when necessary. A couple of minutes every 20–60 minutes is recommended.
	15 minutes Z4		1 & 2 at Z3			
	After completing the effort, continue to the top of the hill or to an appropriate point that will allow an approx. 80-minute run. Following the effort continue at a Z2 intensity.		3–7 at Z4			Cool down
			All on a 4-minute easy Z1 descent			10 minutes easy Z1 running
	On the descent target a Z2 intensity where possible; however, be aware that you will likely also spend considerable time in Z1 and this is fine		This means that you will not quite return to your start point during this time and so will gradually make it further and further up the hill.			
	Hint: as per the 15/10/5 run, it is recommended that you start at the lower end of Z4 for the first 15-minute block. You can then increase the intensity towards the upper end of Z4 over the subsequent 15-minute block if needed. But do not aim to go above Z4.		Cool down			
	Cool down		10 minutes easy Z1 running			
	10 minutes easy Z1 running		Walk & stretch as needed			
	Walk & stretch as needed					

245

WEEK 19: 6 WEEKS TO RACE DAY – BUILD PHASE 2

Monday	Tuesday	Wednesday	Thursday	Friday	Saturday	Sunday
Day off	**Full hill 1 x 30 minutes** Total time: 80–90 minutes *Warm-up* 10 minutes Z1 building to Z2 2 x 3 minutes building over the 3 minutes from Z2 to Z4 *Main set* 1 x 30-minute Z4 uphill effort After completing the effort, continue to the top of the hill or to an appropriate point that will allow an approx. 80-minute run. Following the effort continue at a Z2 intensity. On the descent target a Z2 intensity where possible; however, be aware that you will likely also spend considerable time in Z1 and this is fine *Hint: as per the 15/10/5 run, it is recommended that you start at the lower end of Z4 for the first 15-minute block. You can then increase the intensity towards the upper end of Z4 over the subsequent 15-minute block if needed. But do not aim to go above Z4.* *Cool down* 10 minutes easy Z1 running Walk & stretch as needed	**Easy recovery run** 40 minutes Z2 Spend the first 10 minutes building to Z2	**Hill reps 8 x 6 minutes** Total time: approx. 100 minutes *Warm-up* 10 minutes Z1 building to Z2 4 x 1-minute strides on a 1-minute easy jogging recovery 2 minutes Z2 *Main set* 8 x 6-minute hill reps: 1 & 2 at Z3 3–8 at Z4 All on a 4-minute easy Z1 descent This means that you will not quite return to your start point during this time and so will gradually make it further and further up the hill *Cool down* 10 minutes easy Z1 running Walk & stretch as needed	**Recovery techniques** 20–30 minutes Refer to Chapter 12	**Soul run – trail** 2 hours Aim to gradually build into your running over the first 10 minutes	**Race simulation day** Long run 6 hours *Warm-up* 10 minutes Z1 10 minutes building to Z2 *Main set* Aim to hold a Z1/Z2 effort – where possible target Z2 Include walk breaks when necessary. A couple of minutes every 20–60 minutes is recommended. *Cool down* 10 minutes easy Z1 running

WEEK 20: 5 WEEKS TO RACE DAY – BUILD PHASE 2 (RECOVERY WEEK)

Monday	Tuesday	Wednesday	Thursday	Friday	Saturday	Sunday
Day off	**Easy strides**	**Day off**	**Hill reps 8 x 6 minutes**	**Recovery techniques**	**Soul run – trail**	**Long run**
Schedule a remedial massage if possible	Total time: 50 minutes		Total time: approx. 100 minutes	20–30 minutes	2 hours	4.5 hours
	Warm-up		*Warm-up*	Refer to Chapter 12	Aim to gradually build into your running over the first 10 minutes	*Warm-up*
	10 minutes Z1		10 minutes Z1 building to Z2			10 minutes Z1
	10 minutes Z2		4 x 1-minute strides on a 1-minute easy jogging recovery			10 minutes building to Z2
	Main set		2 minutes Z2			*Main set*
	10 x 1-minute strides		*Main set*			Aim to hold a Z1/Z2 effort – where possible target Z2
	Complete 10 x 1-minute strides at Z3 on a 1-minute Z2 recovery. Try to run to feel and keep the strides comfortable and easy.		8 x 6 minute hill reps:			Include walk breaks when necessary. A couple of minutes every 20–60 minutes is recommended.
			1 & 2 at Z3			
			3–8 at Z4			
	Cool down		All on a 4-minute easy Z1 descent			*Cool down*
	10 minutes easy Z1 running		This means that you will not quite return to your start point during this time and so will gradually make it further and further up the hill			10 minutes easy Z1 running
	Walk & stretch as needed		*Cool down*			
	*If you are feeling more recovery is required, change this set to a 30-minute Z2 recovery run		10 minutes easy Z1 running			
			Walk & stretch as needed			

WEEK 21: 4 WEEKS TO RACE DAY – PEAK WEEK)

Monday	Tuesday	Wednesday	Thursday	Friday	Saturday	Sunday
Day off	**Fitness test No 2 – 60-minute aerobic threshold test** Total time: 90 minutes Refer to Chapter 4	Day off	**Soul run – trail** 40 minutes Aim to gradually build into your running over the first 10 minutes	**Recovery techniques** 20–30 minutes Refer to Chapter 12	**Race simulation** 5 hours *Warm-up* 10 minutes Z1 10 minutes building to Z2 *Main set* Aim to hold a Z1/Z2 effort – where possible target Z2 Include walk breaks when necessary. A couple of minutes every 20–60 minutes is recommended. *Cool down* 10 minutes easy Z1 running	**Race simulation** 5 hours *Warm-up* 10 minutes Z1 10 minutes building to Z2 *Main set* Aim to hold a Z1/Z2 effort – where possible target Z2 Include walk breaks when necessary. A couple of minutes every 20–60 minutes is recommended. *Cool down* 10 minutes easy Z1 running

WEEK 22: 3 WEEKS TO RACE DAY (REDUCED WEEK)

Monday	Tuesday	Wednesday	Thursday	Friday	Saturday	Sunday
Walk	Day off	Easy recovery run	Soul run – trail	Recovery techniques	Hill reps 3 x 6/4 minutes	Long run (short)
20–30 minutes	20–30 minute Walk	20 minutes Z2	80 minutes	20–30 minutes	Total time: approx. 80 minutes	90 minutes
Stretch as needed		Spend the first 10 minutes building to Z2	Aim to gradually build into your running over the first 10 minutes	Refer to Chapter 12	*Warm-up*	*Warm-up*
Schedule a remedial massage if possible			If needed this can also be changed to an easy recovery run		10 minutes Z1 building to Z2	10 minutes Z1
					4 x 1-minute strides on a 1-minute easy jogging recovery	10 minutes building to Z2
					2 minutes Z2	*Main set*
					Main set	Aim to hold a Z1/Z2 effort – where possible target Z2
					3 x 12 minutes: 6 minutes Z3 into 4 minutes Z4 on a 4-minute easy Z1 descent. Turn and repeat.	Include walk breaks when necessary. A couple of minutes every 20–60 minutes is recommended.
					This means that you will not quite return to your start point during this time and so will gradually make it further and further up the hill	Include one 30-minute segment of Z3 running. Aim to complete this segment on a prolonged uphill section if possible.
					Cool down	*Cool down*
					10 minutes easy Z1 running	10 minutes easy Z1 running
					Walk & stretch as needed	
					Visualisation session	

WEEK 23: 2 WEEKS TO RACE DAY – TAPER 2

Monday	Tuesday	Wednesday	Thursday	Friday	Saturday	Sunday
Day off	**Fitness test No. 3** Refer to Chapter 4 Alternatively last intensity session as below **Hill reps 3 x 8/4 minutes** Total time: approx. 80 minutes *Warm-up* 10 minutes Z1 building to Z2 4 x 1-minute strides on a 1-minute easy jogging recovery 2 minutes Z2 *Main set* 3 x 12 minutes: 8 minutes Z3 into 4 minutes Z4 on a 4-minute easy Z1 descent. Turn and repeat. This means that you will not quite return to your start point during this time and so will gradually make it further and further up the hill *Cool down* 10 minutes easy Z1 running Walk & stretch as needed **Visualisation session**	**Day off** Walk as needed	**Easy recovery run** 30 minutes Z2 Try to spend the first 10 minutes building to Z2 **Visualisation session**	**Recovery techniques** 20–30 minutes Refer to Chapter 12	**Soul run – trail** 1 hour Aim to gradually build into your running over the first 10 minutes	**Long run (short)** 90 minutes *Warm-up* 10 minutes Z1 10 minutes building to Z2 *Main set* Aim to hold a Z1/Z2 effort – where possible target Z2 Include walk breaks when necessary. A couple of minutes every 20–60 minutes is recommended. Include one 30-minute segment of Z3 running. Aim to complete this segment on a prolonged uphill section if possible. *Cool down* 10 minutes easy Z1 running

WEEK 24: 1 WEEK TO RACE DAY – TAPER 1 (RACE WEEK)

Monday	Tuesday	Wednesday	Thursday	Friday	Saturday	Sunday
Travel followed by a short 20 minute walk	**Easy recovery run** 30 minutes Easy Z1/ Z2 run & stretching Massage if needed (recommended) but the massage must occur after the run	**Easy run** 40 minutes with short intensity segments Warm-up 10 minutes Z1 building to Z2 4 x 1-minute strides on a 1-minute easy jogging recovery 2 minutes Z2 Main set 4 x 2 minutes Z3 on a 1-minute Z2 recovery Cool down 5–10 minutes easy Z1 **Visualisation session**	**Easy recovery run** 20 minutes Z1/Z2 *Stretching* Carbohydrate-rich meal for dinner	**Day off** If you can cope, or very easy 20-minute run Event check-in and race briefing CHO loading **Optional visualisation session**	**Race day – the ultra graduation** You have done the work, trust yourself, believe in yourself and your ability. You will do great. **Time to smash your 100km ultramarathon**	**Party time & recovery time**

APPENDIX 2: PROGRAM 2

24 WEEKS TO 100KM, WITH 50KM ULTRA RACE IN THE LEAD-UP AND A SATURDAY LONG RUN

This program is ideal for somebody who wishes to complete a major race as part of the preparation for their 100km ultra.

4 DAYS RUNNING/WEEK

WEEK 1: 24 WEEKS TO RACE DAY – BASE PHASE 1

Monday	Tuesday	Wednesday	Thursday	Friday	Saturday	Sunday
Easy, medium, hard Total time: 60 minutes *Warm-up* 10 minutes Z1 building to Z2 2 x 3 minutes building over the 3 minutes from Z2 to Z4 4 minutes Z2 *Main set* **2 (3 x 5 minutes)** 1. 5 minutes easy 2. 5 minutes medium 3. 5 minutes hard Repeat for a total of two reps *Cool down* 10 minutes easy Z1 running Walk & stretch as needed	**Day off** Having hit the ground running, today it is recommended that you look through the remainder of the first week of training and refer to the intensity guide to ensure success with the remainder of the running week!	**4/3/2/1 fartlek set** Total time: 60 minutes *Warm-up* 10 minutes Z1 building to Z2 4 x 1-minute strides on a 1-minute easy jogging recovery 2 minutes Z2 *Main set* This main set is all about starting to learn your zones and how to vary your pace to match each. As you shift to a higher zone you should be running just a little harder. 4 minutes Z2 3 minutes Z3 2 minutes Z4 1 minute Z5b Repeat the main set x 3 *Cool down* 10 minutes easy Z1 running Walk & stretch as needed	**Soul run – trail** 1 hour 30 minutes Aim to gradually build into your running over the first 10 minutes	**Recovery day**	**Long run – trail** 2 hours 20 minutes *Warm-up* 10 minutes Z1 10 minutes building to Z2 *Main set* Aim to hold a Z1/Z2 effort - where possible target Z2. Include walk breaks when necessary. A couple of minutes every 20–60 minutes is recommended. *Cool down* 10 minutes easy Z1 running	**Day off**

WEEK 2: 23 WEEKS TO RACE DAY – BASE PHASE 1

Monday	Tuesday	Wednesday	Thursday	Friday	Saturday	Sunday
Descending pyramid	Day off	**Fitness test No 1 – 30 minute time trial**	**Soul run – trail**	**Recovery techniques**	**Long run – trail**	Day off
Total time: 62 minutes		Total time: 70 minutes	1 hour 30 minutes	20-30 minutes	2 hours 30 minutes	
Warm-up		Refer to Chapter 4	Aim to gradually build into your running over the first 10 minutes.	Refer to Chapter 12	*Warm-up*	
10 minutes Z1 building to Z2					10 minutes Z1	
2 x 3 minutes building over the 3 minutes from Z2 to Z4					10 minutes building to Z2	
4 minutes Z2 running					*Main set*	
Main set					Aim to hold a Z1/Z2 effort – where possible target Z2	
This set is a pyramid set where the recovery is half the time of the work interval. Aim to complete the recovery component at Z2 intensity.					Include walk breaks when necessary. A couple of minutes every 20–60 minutes is recommended.	
6 minutes Z3, 3 minutes Z2					*Cool down*	
5 minutes Z4, 2.5 minutes Z2					10 minutes easy Z1 running	
4 minutes Z4, 2 minutes Z2						
3 minutes Z5a, 90 seconds Z2						
2 minutes Z5b, 60 seconds Z2						
1 minute Z5b, 30 seconds Z2						
Cool down						
10 minutes easy Z1 running						
Walk & stretch as needed						

WEEK 3: 22 WEEKS TO RACE DAY – BASE PHASE 1

Monday	Tuesday	Wednesday	Thursday	Friday	Saturday	Sunday
Four squared	Day off	**Fitness test No 2 – 60 minute aerobic threshold test**	**Soul run – trail**	**Recovery techniques**	**Long run – trail**	Day off
Total time: 61 minutes		Total time: 90 minutes	1 hour 30 minutes	20–30 minutes	2 hours 40 minutes	
Warm-up		Refer to Chapter 4	Aim to gradually build into your running over the first 10 minutes	Refer to Chapter 12	*Warm-up*	
10 minutes Z1 building to Z2					10 minutes Z1	
2 x 3 minutes building over the 3 minutes from Z2 to Z4					10 minutes building to Z2	
4 minutes Z2 running					*Main set*	
15 minutes Z2 running					Aim to hold a Z1/Z2 effort – where possible target Z2	
Main set					Include walk breaks when necessary. A couple of minutes every 20–60 minutes is recommended.	
4 x 4 minutes					*Cool down*	
Each 4-minute block is broken into 1/2/1: the first minute is Z1/2, the next two minutes are Z4 and the final minute is Z5b					10 minutes easy Z1 running	
Cool down						
10 minutes easy Z1 running						
Walk & stretch as needed						

WEEK 4: 21 WEEKS TO RACE DAY – BASE PHASE 1 (RECOVERY WEEK)

Monday	Tuesday	Wednesday	Thursday	Friday	Saturday	Sunday
Easy strides	**Recovery day**	**Fitness test No 3 – uphill time trial**	**Soul run – trail**	**Recovery techniques**	**Long run – trail**	Day off
Total time: 50 minutes	Schedule a remedial massage if possible	Refer to Chapter 4	1 hour 40 minutes	20–30 minutes	2 hours 50 minutes	
Warm-up		*If an additional day of rest is required, shift this set to Saturday and remove the Saturday soul run. Instead, complete an easy 30-minute Z2 recovery run.*	Aim to gradually build into your running over the first 10 minutes	Refer to Chapter 12	*Warm-up*	
10 minutes Z1					10 minutes Z1	
10 minutes Z2					10 minutes building to Z2	
Main set					*Main set*	
10 x 1-minute strides.					Aim to hold a Z1/Z2 effort – where possible target Z2	
Complete 10 x 1-minute strides at Z3 on a 1-minute Z2 recovery.					Include walk breaks when necessary. A couple of minutes every 20–60 minutes is recommended.	
Try to run according to feel and keep the strides comfortable and easy					Include one 30-minute segment of Z3 running. Aim to complete this segment on a prolonged uphill if possible.	
Cool down					*Cool down*	
10 minutes easy Z1 running					10 minutes easy Z1 running	
Walk & stretch as needed						
If you feel more recovery is required, change this set to a 30-minute Z2 recovery run						

257

WEEK 5: 20 WEEKS TO RACE DAY – BASE PHASE 2

Monday	Tuesday	Wednesday	Thursday	Friday	Saturday	Sunday
12 minute ramps	Day off	**4/3/2/1 max intensity builds**	**Soul run – trail**	**Recovery techniques**	**Long run – trail**	Day off
Total time: 69 minutes		Total Time: 60 minutes	1 hour 50 minutes	20–30 minutes	3 hours	
Warm-up		*Warm-up*	Aim to gradually build into your running over the first 10 minutes	Refer to Chapter 12	*Warm-up*	
10 minutes Z1 building to Z2		10 minutes Z1 building to Z2			10 minutes Z1	
2 x 3 minutes building over the 3 minutes from Z2 to Z4		4 x 1-minute strides on a 1-minute easy jogging recovery			10 minutes building to Z2	
Main set		12 minutes Z2			*Main set*	
3 x 12-minute builds:		*Main set*			Aim to hold a Z1/Z2 effort – where possible target Z2	
3 minutes Z2		Take the first 30 seconds to build into each of the efforts.			Include walk breaks when necessary. A couple of minutes every 20–60 minutes is recommended.	
3 minutes Z3		4 minutes Z5b 4 minute Z2				
3 minutes Z4		3 minutes Z5b 3 minute Z2			*Cool down*	
3 minutes Z5b		2 minutes Z5b 2 minute Z2			10 minutes easy Z1 running	
At the conclusion of each block include a 1-minute walk		1 minute Z5b 1 minute Z2				
Cool down		*Cool down*				
10 minutes easy Z1 running		10 minutes easy Z1 running				
Walk & stretch as needed		Walk & stretch as needed				

WEEK 6: 19 WEEKS TO RACE DAY – BASE PHASE 2

Monday	Tuesday	Wednesday	Thursday	Friday	Saturday	Sunday
Pyramid fartlek	Day off	**Hard/easy**	**Soul run – trail**	**Recovery techniques**	**Long run – trail**	Day off
Total time: 67 minutes		Total time: 60 minutes	2 hours	20–30 minutes	3 hours 10 minutes	
Warm-up		*Warm-up*	Aim to gradually build into your running over the first 10 minutes	Refer to Chapter 12	*Warm-up*	
10 minutes Z1 building to Z2		10 minutes Z1 building to Z2			10 minutes Z1	
2 x 3 minutes building over the 3 minutes from Z2 to Z4		4 x 1-minute strides on a 1-minute easy jogging recovery			10 minutes building to Z2	
Main set		2 minutes Z2			*Main set*	
Complete the following pyramid alternating between Z2 and Z4:		*Main set*			Aim to hold a Z1/Z2 effort – where possible target Z2	
		15 x 1 minutes on a 1-minute Z2 Recovery:			Include walk breaks when necessary. A couple of minutes every 20–60 minutes is recommended.	
4 minutes Z4		1–8 at Z4				
5 minutes Z2		9–15 at Z5a			*Cool down*	
6 minutes Z4		*Cool down*			10 minutes easy Z1 running	
7 minutes Z2		10 minutes easy Z1 running				
6 minutes Z4		Walk & stretch as needed				
5 minutes Z2		Be aware that HR will not respond completely during the efforts so you will have to rely on your feel for your output or RPE				
4 minutes Z4						
Cool down						
10 minutes easy Z1 running						
Walk & stretch as needed						

WEEK 7: 18 WEEKS TO RACE DAY – BASE PHASE 2

Monday	Tuesday	Wednesday	Thursday	Friday	Saturday	Sunday
12 minute ramps	**Day off**	**Pyramid down**	**Soul run – trail**	**Recovery techniques**	**Long run – trail**	**Day off**
Total time: 82 minutes		Total time: Approx. 60 minutes	2 hours 10 minutes	20–30 minutes	3 hours 20 minutes	
Warm-up		*Warm-up*	Aim to gradually build into your running over the first 10 minutes	Refer to Chapter 12	*Warm-up*	
10 minutes Z1 building to Z2		10 minutes Z1 building to Z2			10 minutes Z1	
2 x 3 minutes building over the 3 minutes from Z2 to Z4		4 x 1-minute strides on a 1-minute easy jogging recovery			10 minutes building to Z2	
Main set		2 minutes Z2			*Main set*	
4 x 12 minute builds:		*Main set*			Aim to hold a Z1/Z2 effort – where possible target Z2	
3 minutes Z2		Run straight through:			Include walk breaks when necessary. A couple of minutes every 20–60 minutes is recommended.	
3 minutes Z3		6 minutes Z2 1 minute Z5b				
3 minutes Z4		5 minutes Z2 1 minute Z5b				
3 minutes Z5b		4 minutes Z2 1 minute Z5b			Include one 20-minute segment of Zone 3 running. Aim to complete this segment on a prolonged uphill if possible.	
At the conclusion of each block include a 1-minute walk.		3 minutes Z2 1 minute Z5b				
Cool down		2 minutes Z2 1 minute Z5b			*Cool down*	
10 minutes easy Z1 running		1 minutes Z2 1 minute Z5b			10 minutes easy Z1 running	
Walk & stretch as needed		*Cool down*				
		10 minutes easy Z1 running				
		Walk & stretch as needed				

WEEK 8: 17 WEEKS TO RACE DAY – BASE PHASE 2 (RECOVERY WEEK)

Monday	Tuesday	Wednesday	Thursday	Friday	Saturday	Sunday
6 squared run	**Day off**	**Hill reps 6 x 3 minutes**	**Soul run – trail**	**Recovery techniques**	**Long run – trail**	**Day off**
Total time: 66 minutes	Schedule a remedial massage if possible.	Total time: approx. 75 minutes	2 hour 20 minutes	20–30 minutes	3 hours 30 minutes	
Warm-up		*Warm-up*	Aim to gradually build into your running over the first 10 minutes	Refer to Chapter 12	*Warm-up*	
10 minutes Z1 building to Z2		10 minutes Z1 building to Z2			10 minutes Z1	
2 x 3 minutes building over the 3 minutes from Z2 to Z4		4 x 1-minute strides on a 1-minute easy jogging recovery			10 minutes building to Z2	
Main set		2 minutes Z2			*Main set*	
6 x 6 minutes:		*Main set*			Aim to hold a Z1/Z2 effort – where possible target Z2	
3 minutes Z2		6 x 3 minute hill reps building to Z5b on an easy Z1 descent and 60 seconds RI			Include walk breaks when necessary. A couple of minutes every 20–60 minutes is recommended.	
2 minutes Z3		This means that you run the hill or part of a hill from a chosen start point for 3 minutes duration. At this point hit the lap button on your watch. Turn for an easy recovery jog down the hill.			Include one 30 minute segment of Zone 3 running. Aim to complete this segment on a prolonged uphill, if possible.	
1 minute Z4		Upon reaching your start point have a 60 second rest and then repeat. Complete this for a total of 6 reps.			*Cool down*	
Cool down		*Cool down*			10 minutes easy Z1 running	
10 minutes easy Z1 running		10 minutes easy Z1 running				
Walk & stretch as needed		Walk & stretch as needed				
*If you feel more recovery is required, change this set to a 30-minute Z2 recovery run						

WEEK 9: 16 WEEKS TO RACE DAY – BASE PHASE 3

Monday	Tuesday	Wednesday	Thursday	Friday	Saturday	Sunday
Uphill effort – 15 minutes	Day off	**Hill reps 7 x 3 minutes**	**Soul run – trail**	**Recovery techniques**	**Long run – trail**	Day off
Total time: 80 minutes		Total time: approx. 80 minutes	2 hours 30 minutes	20-30 minutes	3 hours 40 minutes	
Warm-up		*Warm-up*	Aim to gradually build into your running over the first 10 minutes	Refer to Chapter 12	*Warm-up*	
10 minutes Z1 building to Z2		10 minutes Z1 building to Z2			10 minutes Z1	
2 x 3 minutes building over the 3 minutes from Z2 to Z4		4 x 1-minute strides on a 1-minute easy jogging recovery			10 minutes building to Z2	
10 minutes Z2		2 minutes Z2			*Main set*	
Main set		*Main set*			Aim to hold a Z1/Z2 effort – where possible target Z2	
1 x 15 minutes uphill effort Z4		7 x 3-minute hill reps building to Z5b on an easy Z1 descent and 60 seconds RI			Include walk breaks when necessary. A couple of minutes every 20-60 minutes is recommended.	
After completing the effort, continue to the top of the hill or to an appropriate point that will allow an approx. 80-minute run. Following the effort, continue at a Z2 intensity.		As per last week, but this time adding another rep			*Cool down*	
On the descent target a Z2 intensity where possible; however, be aware that you will likely also spend considerable time in Z1 and this is fine		*Cool down*			10 minutes easy Z1 running	
		10 minutes easy Z1 running				
Cool down		Walk & stretch as needed				
10 minutes easy Z1 running						
Walk & stretch as needed						

Monday	Tuesday	Wednesday	Thursday	Friday	Saturday	Sunday
Uphill effort – 20 minutes Total time: 80 minutes *Warm-up* 10 minutes Z1 building to Z2 2 x 3 minutes building over the 3 minutes from Z2 to Z4 10 minutes Z2 *Main set* 1 x 20 minutes uphill effort Z4 After completing the effort, continue to the top of the hill or to an appropriate point that will allow an approx. 80 minute run. Following the effort continue at a Z2 intensity. On the descent, target a Z2 intensity where possible, however, be aware that you will likely also spend considerable time in Z1 and this is fine *Cool down* 10 minutes easy Z1 running Walk & stretch as needed	Day off	**Hill reps 5 x 5 minutes** Total time: approx. 80 minutes *Warm-up* 10 minutes Z1 building to Z2 4 x 1-minute strides on a 1-minute easy jogging recovery 2 minutes Z2 *Main set* 5 x 5 minute hill reps building to Z5a on an easy Z1 descent and 60 seconds RI *Cool down* 10 minutes easy Z1 running Walk & stretch as needed	**Soul run – trail** 2 hours 40 minutes Aim to gradually build into your running over the first 10 minutes	**Recovery techniques** 20–30 minutes Refer to Chapter 12	**Long Run - Trail** 3 hours 50 minutes *Warm-up* 10 minutes Z1 10 minutes building to Z2 *Main set* Aim to hold a Z1/Z2 effort – where possible target Z2 Include walk breaks when necessary. A couple of minutes every 20-60 minutes is recommended. *Cool down* 10 minutes easy Z1 running	Day off

PROGRAM TWO

WEEK 11: 14 WEEKS TO RACE DAY – BASE PHASE 3

Monday	Tuesday	Wednesday	Thursday	Friday	Saturday	Sunday
Uphill effort – 3 x 10 minute	Day off	**Hill reps 6 x 5 minutes**	**Soul run – trail**	**Recovery techniques**	**Long run – trail**	Day off
Total time: 80–90 minutes		Total time: approx. 80 minutes	2 hours 50 minutes	20–30 minutes	3 hours	
Warm-up		*Warm-up*	Aim to gradually build into your running over the first 10 minutes	Refer to Chapter 12	*Warm-up*	
10 minutes Z1 building to Z2		10 minutes Z1 building to Z2			10 minutes Z1	
2 x 3 minutes building over the 3 minutes from Z2 to Z4		4 x 1-minute strides on a 1-minute easy jogging recovery			10 minutes building to Z2	
Main set		2 minutes Z2			*Main set*	
3 x 10 minutes uphill effort:		*Main set*			Aim to hold a Z1/Z2 effort – where possible target Z2	
1 x 10 minutes Z3		6 x 5-minute hill reps Z4 on an easy Z1 descent			Include walk breaks when necessary. A couple of minutes every 20–60 minutes is recommended.	
2 x 10 minutes Z4		*Cool down*			*Cool down*	
All on a 4 minute Z2 recovery		10 minutes easy Z1 running			10 minutes easy Z1 running	
After completing the effort, continue to the top of the hill or to an appropriate point that will allow an approx. 80 minute run. Following the effort continue at a Z2 intensity.		Walk & stretch as needed				
On the descent target a Z2 intensity where possible; however, be aware that you will likely also spend considerable time in Z1 and this is fine						
Cool down						
10 minutes easy Z1 running						
Walk & stretch as needed						

WEEK 12: 13 WEEKS TO RACE DAY – BASE PHASE 3 (RECOVERY WEEK)

Monday	Tuesday	Wednesday	Thursday	Friday	Saturday	Sunday
Easy recovery run	**Day off**	**Soul run – trail**	**Easy run**	**Recovery techniques**	**50km ultramarathon**	**Day off**
Total time: 60 minutes	Schedule a remedial massage if possible	60 minutes	40 minutes with short intensity segments	20–30 minutes	Make sure to formulate your pacing plan and nutrition plan	Walk 20–30 minutes
Warm-up:		Aim to gradually build into your running over the first 10 minutes	*Warm-up*	Refer to Chapter 12		
10 minutes Z1			10 minutes Z1 building to Z2			
10 minutes building to Z2			4 x 1-minute strides on a 1-minute easy jogging recovery			
Easy 30 minute Z2 run.						
This can be completed on the trails or road.			2 minutes Z2			
Cool down			Main set			
10 minutes easy Z1			4 x 2 minutes Z3 on a 1-minute Z2 recovery			
Visualisation session			Cool down			
			5–10 minutes easy Z1			
			Visualisation session			

WEEK 13: 12 WEEKS TO RACE DAY – BUILD PHASE 1

Monday	Tuesday	Wednesday	Thursday	Friday	Saturday	Sunday
Walk	Day off	**Easy recovery run**	**Soul run – trail**	**Recovery techniques**	**Long run – trail**	Day off
20–30 minutes		Total time: 30 minutes	50 minutes	20–30 minutes	1 hours 10 minutes	
Recovery techniques		*Warm-up:*	Aim to gradually build into your running over the first 10 minutes	Refer to Chapter 12	*Warm-up*	
20–30 minutes		10 minutes Z1			10 minutes Z1	
Refer to Chapter 12		20 minutes Z2			10 minutes building to Z2	
		Cool down			*Main set*	
		10 minutes easy Z1			Aim to hold a Z1/Z2 effort – where possible target Z2	
					Include walk breaks when necessary. A couple of minutes every 20–60 minutes is recommended.	
					Cool down	
					10 minutes easy Z1 running	

WEEK 14: 11 WEEKS TO RACE DAY – BUILD PHASE 1

Monday	Tuesday	Wednesday	Thursday	Friday	Saturday	Sunday
Hill reps 2 x 8/4 minutes	**Day off**	**Uphill effort – 15/10/5 minute**	**Soul run – trail**	**Recovery techniques**	**Long run – trail**	**Day off**
Total time: approx. 70 minutes		Total time: 80–90 minutes	2 hours 30 minutes	20–30 minutes	4 hours 00 minutes	
Warm-up		*Warm-up*	Aim to gradually build into your running over the first 10 minutes	Refer to Chapter 12	*Warm-up*	
10 minutes Z1 building to Z2		10 minutes Z1 building to Z2			10 minutes Z1	
4 x 1-minute strides on a 1-minute easy jogging recovery		2 x 3 minutes building over the 3 minutes from Z2 to Z4			10 minutes building to Z2	
2 minutes Z2		*Main set*			*Main set*	
Main set		1 x 15 minutes Z3			Aim to hold a Z1/Z2 effort – where possible target Z2	
2 x 12 minutes as 8 minutes Z3 into 4 minutes Z4 on a 4-minute easy Z1 descent. Turn and repeat.		1 x 10 minutes Z4				
		1 x 5 minutes Z4			Include walk breaks when necessary. A couple of minutes every 20–60 minutes is recommended.	
This means that you will not quite return to your start point during this time and so will gradually make it further and further up the hill		All on a 4=minute Z2 recovery				
		After completing the effort continue to the top of the hill or to an appropriate point that will allow an approx. 80 minute run. Following the effort continue at a Z2 intensity.			*Cool down*	
Cool down					10 minutes easy Z1 running	
10 minutes easy Z1 running		On the descent target a Z2 intensity where possible; however, be aware that you will likely also spend considerable time in Z1 and this is fine				
Walk & stretch as needed		*Cool down*				
		10 minutes easy Z1 running				
		Walk & stretch as needed				

WEEK 15: 10 WEEKS TO RACE DAY – BUILD PHASE 1

Monday	Tuesday	Wednesday	Thursday	Friday	Saturday	Sunday
Uphill effort – 15/10/5 minute	Day off	**Hill reps 3 x 8/4 minutes**	**Soul run – trail**	**Recovery techniques**	**Long run – trail**	Day off
Total time: 80–90 minutes		Total time: approx. 80 minutes	3 hours	20–30 minutes	5 hours	
Warm-up		*Warm-up*	Aim to gradually build into your running over the first 10 minutes	Refer to Chapter 12	*Warm-up*	
10 minutes Z1 building to Z2		10 minutes Z1 building to Z2			10 minutes Z1	
2 x 3 minutes building over the 3 minutes from Z2 to Z4		4 x 1-minute strides on a 1-minute easy jogging recovery			10 minutes building to Z2	
Main set		2 minutes Z2			*Main set*	
15/10/5 minutes uphill effort as follows:		*Main set*			Aim to hold a Z1/Z2 effort – where possible target Z2	
15 minute Z4 on a 6-minute Z2 recovery		3 x 12 minutes as 8 minutes Z3 into 4 minutes Z4				
10 minute Z4 on a 4-minute Z2 recovery		All on a 4-minute easy Z1 descent. Turn and repeat.			Include walk breaks when necessary. A couple of minutes every 20–60 minutes is recommended.	
5 minute Z4 followed by a 2-minute walk for a job well done		This means that you will not quite return to your start point during this time and so will gradually make it further and further up the hill				
After completing the effort continue to the top of the hill or to an appropriate point that will allow an approx. 80 minute run. Following the effort continue at a Z2 intensity.		*Cool down*			*Cool down*	
On the descent target a Z2 intensity where possible; however, be aware that you will likely also spend considerable time in Z1 and this is fine		10 minutes easy Z1 running			10 minutes easy Z1 running	
Hint: it is recommended that you start at the lower end of Z4 for the first 15-minute block. You can then increase the intensity towards the upper end of Z4 over the 10 and 5-minute period if needed.		Walk & stretch as needed				
Cool down						
10 minutes easy Z1 running						
Walk & stretch as needed						

WEEK 16: 9 WEEKS TO RACE DAY – BUILD PHASE 2 (RECOVERY WEEK)

Monday	Tuesday	Wednesday	Thursday	Friday	Saturday	Sunday
Easy strides	**Day off**	**Hill Reps 6 x 6 minutes**	**Soul run – trail**	**Recovery techniques**	**Long run – trail**	Day off
Total time: 50 minutes	Schedule a remedial massage if possible	Total time: approx. 80 minutes	3 hours	20–30 minutes	5 hours 15 minutes	
Warm-up		*Warm-up*	Aim to gradually build into your running over the first 10 minutes	Refer to Chapter 12	*Warm-up*	
10 minutes Z1		10 minutes Z1 building to Z2			10 minutes Z1	
10 minutes Z2		4 x 1-minute strides on a 1-minute easy jogging recovery			10 minutes building to Z2	
Main set		2 minutes Z2			*Main set*	
10 x 1-minute strides		*Main set*			Aim to hold a Z1/Z2 effort – where possible target Z2	
Complete 10 x1-minute strides Z3 on a 1-minute Z2 recovery.		6 x 6 minute hill reps:			Include walk breaks when necessary. A couple of minutes every 20–60 minutes is recommended.	
Try to run on feel and keep the strides comfortable and easy.		1 & 2 at Z3				
		3–6 at Z4			*Cool down*	
Cool down		All on a 4-minute easy Z1 descent			10 minutes easy Z1 running	
10 minutes easy Z1 running		This means that you will not quite return to your start point during this time and so will gradually make it further and further up the hill				
Walk & stretch as needed		*Cool down*				
If you're feeling more recovery is required, change this set to a 30-minute Z2 recovery run		10 minutes easy Z1 running				
		Walk & stretch as needed				

WEEK 17: 8 WEEKS TO RACE DAY – BUILD PHASE 2

Monday	Tuesday	Wednesday	Thursday	Friday	Saturday	Sunday
Split the hill Total time: 80–90 minutes *Warm-up* 10 minutes Z1 building to Z2 2 x 3 minutes building over the 3 minutes from Z2 to Z4 *Main set* 2 x 15 minute uphill efforts: 1 x 15 minutes Z4 on a 6-minute Z2 recovery 1 x 15 minutes Z4 After completing the effort continue to the top of the hill or to an appropriate point that will allow an approx. 80-minute run. Following the effort continue at a Z2 intensity. On the descent target a Z2 intensity where possible; however, be aware that you will likely also spend considerable time in Z1 and this is fine *Hint: it is recommended that you start at the lower end of Z4 for the first 15-minute block. You can then increase the intensity towards the upper end of Z4 over the 10 and 5-minute period if needed.* *Cool down* 10 minutes easy Z1 running Walk & stretch as needed	Day off	**Hill reps 7 x 6 minutes** Total time: approx. 90 minutes *Warm-up* 10 minutes Z1 building to Z2 4 x 1-minute strides on a 1-minute easy jogging recovery 2 minutes Z2 *Main set* 7 x 6 minute hill reps: 1 & 2 at Z3 3–7 at Z4 All on a 4-minute easy Z1 descent This means that you will not quite return to your start point during this time and so will gradually make it further and further up the hill *Cool down* 10 minutes easy Z1 running Walk & stretch as needed	**Soul run – trail** 3 hours Aim to gradually build into your running over the first 10 minutes	**Recovery techniques** 20–30 minutes Refer to Chapter 12	**Long run – trail** 5 hours 30 minutes *Warm-up* 10 minutes Z1 10 minutes building to Z2 *Main set* Aim to hold a Z1/Z2 effort – where possible target Z2 Include walk breaks when necessary. A couple of minutes every 20–60 minutes is recommended. *Cool down* 10 minutes easy Z1 running	Day off

Monday	Tuesday	Wednesday	Thursday	Friday	Saturday	Sunday
Split the hill 2 x 15 minutes	Day off	**Hill reps 7x 6 minutes**	**Soul run – trail**	**Recovery techniques**	**Long run – trail**	Day off
Total time: 80 minutes		Total time: approx. 90 minutes	4 hours	20–30 minutes	4 hours	
Warm-up		Warm-up	Aim to gradually build into your running over the first 10 minutes	Refer to Chapter 12	Warm-up	
10 minutes Z1 building to Z2		10 minutes Z1 building to Z2			10 minutes Z1	
2 x 3 minutes building over the 3 minutes from Z2 to Z4		4 x 1-minute strides on a 1-minute easy jogging recovery			10 minutes building to Z2	
Main set		Main set			Main set	
2 x 15 minute uphill efforts as follows:		2 minutes Z2			Aim to hold a Z1/Z2 effort – where possible target Z2	
15 minutes Z4 on a 5-minute Z2 recovery		7 x 6 minute hill reps:			Include walk breaks when necessary. A couple of minutes every 20–60 minutes is recommended.	
15 minutes Z4		1 & 2 at Z3			Cool down	
After completing the effort continue to the top of the hill or to an appropriate point that will allow an approx. 80 minute run. Following the effort continue at a Z2 intensity.		3–7 at Z4			10 minutes easy Z1 running	
On the descent target a Z2 intensity where possible; however, be aware that you will likely also spend considerable time in Z1 and this is fine		All on a 4 minute easy Z1 descent				
Hint: as per the 15/10/5 run, it is recommended that you start at the lower end of Z4 for the first 15-minute block. You can then increase the intensity towards the upper end of Z4 over the subsequent 15-minute block if needed. But do not aim to go above Z4.		This means that you will not quite return to your start point during this time and so will gradually make it further and further up the hill				
Cool down		Cool down				
10 minutes easy Z1 running		10 minutes easy Z1 running				
Walk & stretch as needed		Walk & stretch as needed				

PROGRAM TWO

WEEK 19: 6 WEEKS TO RACE DAY – BUILD PHASE 2

Monday	Tuesday	Wednesday	Thursday	Friday	Saturday	Sunday
Full hill 1 x 30 minutes	Day off	**Hill reps 8 x 6 minutes**	**Soul run – trail**	**Recovery techniques**	**Race simulation day**	Day off
Total time: 80–90 minutes		Total time: approx. 100 minutes	2 hours	20–30 minutes	**Long run**	
Warm-up		*Warm-up*	Aim to gradually build into your running over the first 10 minutes	Refer to Chapter 12	6 hours	
10 minutes Z1 building to Z2		10 minutes Z1 building to Z2			*Warm-up*	
2 x 3 minutes building over the 3 minutes from Z2 to Z4		4 x 1-minute strides on a 1-minute easy jogging recovery			10 minutes Z1	
Main set		2 minutes Z2			10 minutes building to Z2	
1 x 30-minute Z4 uphill effort		*Main set*			*Main set*	
After completing the effort continue to the top of the hill or to an appropriate point that will allow an approx. 80-minute run. Following the effort continue at a Z2 intensity.		8 x 6-minute hill reps:			Aim to hold a Z1/Z2 effort – where possible target Z2	
		1 & 2 at Z3			Include walk breaks when necessary. A couple of minutes every 20–60 minutes is recommended.	
On the descent target a Z2 intensity where possible; however, be aware that you will likely also spend considerable time in Z1 and this is fine		3–8 at Z4				
		All on a 4-minute easy Z1 descent			*Cool down*	
Hint: as per the 15/10/5 run, it is recommended that you start at the lower end of Z4 for the first 15-minute block. You can then increase the intensity towards the upper end of Z4 over the subsequent 15-minute block if needed. But do not aim to go above Z4.		This means that you will not quite return to your start point during this time and so will gradually make it further and further up the hill			10 minutes easy Z1 running	
Cool down		*Cool down*				
10 minutes easy Z1 running		10 minutes easy Z1 running				
Walk & stretch as needed		Walk & stretch as needed				

WEEK 20: 5 WEEKS TO RACE DAY – BUILD PHASE 2 (RECOVERY WEEK)

Monday	Tuesday	Wednesday	Thursday	Friday	Saturday	Sunday
Easy strides	**Day off**	**Hill reps 8 x 6 minutes**	**Soul run – trail**	**Recovery techniques**	**Long run**	**Day off**
Total time: 50 minutes	Schedule a remedial massage if possible.	Total time: approx. 100 minutes	2 hours	20–30 minutes	4.5 hours	
Warm-up		*Warm-up*	Aim to gradually build into your running over the first 10 minutes	Refer to Chapter 12	*Warm-up*	
10 minutes Z1		10 minutes Z1 building to Z2			10 minutes Z1	
10 minutes Z2		4 x 1-minute strides on a 1-minute easy jogging recovery			10 minutes building to Z2	
Main set		2 minutes Z2			*Main set*	
10 x - minute strides		*Main set*			Aim to hold a Z1/Z2 effort – where possible target Z2	
Complete 10 x 1-minute strides at Z3 on a 1-minute Z2 recovery. Try to run to feel and keep the strides comfortable and easy.		8 x 6 minute hill reps:			Include walk breaks when necessary. A couple of minutes every 20–60 minutes is recommended.	
Cool down		1 & 2 at Z3			*Cool down*	
10 minutes easy Z1 running		3–8 at Z4			10 minutes easy Z1 running	
Walk & stretch as needed		All on a 4-minute easy Z1 descent				
If you are feeling more recovery is required, change this set to a 30-minute Z2 recovery run.		This means that you will not quite return to your start point during this time and so will gradually make it further and further up the hill				
		Cool down				
		10 minutes easy Z1 running				
		Walk & stretch as needed				

WEEK 21: 4 WEEKS TO RACE DAY (PEAK WEEK)

Monday	Tuesday	Wednesday	Thursday	Friday	Saturday	Sunday
Fitness test No 2 – 60 minute aerobic threshold test Total time: 90 minutes Refer to Chapter 4	Day off	**Soul run – trail** 40 minutes Aim to gradually build into your running over the first 10 minutes	**Race simulation** 5 hours *Warm-up* 10 minutes Z1 10 minutes building to Z2 *Main set* Aim to hold a Z1/Z2 effort – where possible target Z2. Include walk breaks when necessary. A couple of minutes every 20–60 minutes is recommended. *Cool down* 10 minutes easy Z1 running	**Recovery techniques** 20–30 minutes Refer to Chapter 12	**Race simulation** 5 hours *Warm-up* 10 minutes Z1 10 minutes building to Z2 *Main set* Aim to hold a Z1/Z2 effort – where possible target Z2 Include walk breaks when necessary. A couple of minutes every 20–60 minutes is recommended. *Cool down* 10 minutes easy Z1 running	Day off

WEEK 22: 3 WEEKS TO RACE DAY (REDUCED WEEK)

Monday	Tuesday	Wednesday	Thursday	Friday	Saturday	Sunday
Easy recovery run Total time: 30 minutes *Warm-up:* 10 minutes Z1 20 minutes Z2	Day off	**Soul run – trail** 50 minutes Aim to gradually build into your running over the first 10 minutes If needed this can also changed to an easy recovery run	**Hill reps 3 x 6/4 minutes** Total time: approx. 80 minutes *Warm-up* 10 minutes Z1 building to Z2 4 x 1-minute strides on a 1-minute easy jogging recovery 2 minutes Z2 *Main set* 3 x 12 minutes: 6 minutes Z3 into 4 minutes Z4 on a 4-minute easy Z1 descent. Turn and repeat. This means that you will not quite return to your start point during this time and so will gradually make it further and further up the hill *Cool down* 10 minutes easy Z1 running Walk & stretch as needed **Visualisation session**	**Recovery techniques** 20–30 minutes Refer to Chapter 12	**Long run (short)** 90 minutes *Warm-up* 10 minutes Z1 10 minutes building to Z2 *Main set* Aim to hold a Z1/Z2 effort – where possible target Z2 Include walk breaks when necessary. A couple of minutes every 20–60 minutes is recommended. Include one 30 minute segment of Z3 running. Aim to complete this segment on a prolonged uphill section if possible. *Cool down* 10 minutes easy Z1 running	Day off

WEEK 23: 2 WEEKS TO RACE DAY – TAPER 2

Monday	Tuesday	Wednesday	Thursday	Friday	Saturday	Sunday
Fitness test No 3	**Day off**	**Easy recovery run**	**Soul run – trail**	**Recovery techniques**	**Long run (short)**	Day off
Refer to Chapter 4	Walk as needed	30 minutes Z2	1 hour	20–30 minutes	90 minutes	
Alternatively last intensity session as below		Try to spend the first 10 minutes building to Z2	Aim to gradually build into your running over the first 10 minutes	Refer to Chapter 12	*Warm-up*	
Hill reps 3 x 8/4 minutes		**Visualisation session**			10 minutes Z1	
Total time: approx. 80 minutes					10 minutes building to Z2	
Warm-up					*Main set*	
10 minutes Z1 building to Z2					Aim to hold a Z1/Z2 effort – where possible target Z2	
4 x 1-minute strides on a 1-minute easy jogging recovery					Include walk breaks when necessary. A couple of minutes every 20–60 minutes is recommended.	
2 minutes Z2						
Main set					Include one 30 minute segment of Z3 running. Aim to complete this segment on a prolonged uphill section if possible.	
3 x 12 minutes: 8 minutes Z3 into 4 minutes Z4 on a 4-minute easy Z1 descent. Turn and repeat.						
This means that you will not quite return to your start point during this time and so will gradually make it further and further up the hill					*Cool down*	
Cool down					10 minutes easy Z1 running	
10 minutes easy Z1 running						
Walk & stretch as needed						
Visualisation session						

WEEK 24: 1 WEEK TO RACE DAY – TAPER 1 (RACE WEEK)

Monday	Tuesday	Wednesday	Thursday	Friday	Saturday	Sunday
Easy recovery run	Travel followed by a short 20-minute walk	**Easy run**	**Easy recovery run**	**Day off**	**Race day – the ultra graduation**	**Party time & recovery time**
30 minutes		40 minutes with short intensity segments	20 minutes Z1/Z2	If you can cope, or very easy 20-minute run	You have done the work, trust yourself, believe in yourself and your ability. You will do great.	
Easy Z1/ Z2 run & stretching		*Warm-up*	**Stretching**	Event check-in and race briefing		
Massage if needed (recommended) but the massage must occur after the run		10 minutes Z1 build-ing to Z2	Carbohydrate-rich meal for dinner	CHO loading	**Time to smash your 100km ultra marathon**	
		4 x 1-minute strides on a 1-minute easy jogging recovery		**Optional** visualisation session		
		2 minutes Z2				
		Main set				
		4 x 2 minutes Z3 on a 1-minute Z2 recovery				
		Cool down				
		5–10 minutes easy Z1				
		Visualisation session				

24 WEEKS TO 100KM, WITH A 'WORKING' WEEK LONG RUN ON WEDNESDAY

This is ideal for runners working part-time, especially those with kids.

WEEK 1: 24 WEEKS TO RACE DAY – BASE PHASE 1

Monday	Tuesday	Wednesday	Thursday	Friday	Saturday	Sunday
Easy, medium, hard	**Day off**	**Long run – trail**	**Walk**	**4/3/2/1 fartlek set**	**Soul run – trail**	**Recovery day**
Total time: 60 minutes	Having hit the ground running today it is recommended that you look through the remainder of the first week of training and refer to the intensity guide to ensure success with the remainder of the running week!	2 hours 20 minutes	20-30 minutes	Total time: 60 minutes	1 hour 30 minutes	
Warm-up		*Warm-up*		*Warm-up*	Aim to gradually build into your running over the first 10 minutes	
10 minutes Z1 building to Z2		10 minutes Z1		10 minutes Z1 building to Z2		
2 x 3 minutes building over the 3 minutes from Z2 to Z4		10 minutes building to Z2		4 x 1-minute strides on a 1-minute easy jogging recovery		
4 minutes Z2		*Main set*		2 minutes Z2		
Main set		Aim to hold a Z1/Z2 effort – where possible target Z2		*Main set*		
2 (3 x 5 minutes)		Include walk breaks when necessary. A couple of minutes every 20-60 minutes is recommended.		This main set is all about starting to learn your zones and how to vary your pace to match each. As you shift to a higher zone you should be running just a little harder.		
1. 5 minutes easy		*Cool down*		4 minutes Z2		
2. 5 minutes medium		10 minutes easy Z1 running		3 minutes Z3		
3. 5 minutes hard				2 minutes Z4		
Repeat for a total of two reps				1 minute Z5b		
Cool down				Repeat three times		
10 minutes easy Z1 running				*Cool down*		
Walk & stretch as needed				10 minutes easy Z1 running		
				Walk & stretch as needed		

WEEK 2: 23 WEEKS TO RACE DAY – BASE PHASE 1

Monday	Tuesday	Wednesday	Thursday	Friday	Saturday	Sunday
Descending pyramid	**Walk**	**Long run – trail**	**Recovery techniques**	**Fitness test No 1 – 30 minute time trial**	**Soul run – trail**	**Day off**
Total time: *62 minutes*	20–30 minutes	2 hours 30 minutes	20–30 minutes	Total time: 70 minutes	1 hour 30 minutes	
Warm-up		*Warm-up*	Refer to Chapter 12	Refer to Chapter 4	Aim to gradually build into your running over the first 10 minutes	
10 minutes Z1 building to Z2		10 minutes Z1				
2 x 3 minutes building over the 3 minutes from Z2 to Z4		10 minutes building to Z2				
4 minutes Z2 running		*Main set*				
Main set		Aim to hold a Z1/Z2 effort – where possible target Z2				
This set is a pyramid set where the recovery is half the time of the work interval. Aim to complete the recovery component at Z2 intensity.		Include walk breaks when necessary. A couple of minutes every 20–60 minutes is recommended.				
6 minutes Z3, 3 minutes Z2		*Cool down*				
5 minutes Z4, 2.5 minutes Z2		10 minutes easy Z1 running				
4 minutes Z4, 2 minutes Z2						
3 minutes Z5a, 90 seconds Z2						
2 minutes Z5b, 60 seconds Z2						
1 minute Z5b, 30 seconds Z2						
Cool down						
10 minutes easy Z1 running						
Walk & stretch as needed						

WEEK 3: 22 WEEKS TO RACE DAY – BASE PHASE 1

Monday	Tuesday	Wednesday	Thursday	Friday	Saturday	Sunday
Four squared	**Easy recovery run**	**Long run – trail**	**Recovery techniques**	**Fitness test No 2 – 60 minute aerobic threshold test**	**Soul run – trail**	Day off
Total time: 61 minutes	20 minutes Z2	2 hours 40 minutes	20–30 minutes	Total time: 90 minutes	1 hour 30 minutes	
Warm-up	Spend the first 10 minutes building to Z2	*Warm-up*	Refer to Chapter 12	Refer to Chapter 4	Aim to gradually build into your running over the first 10 minutes	
10 minutes Z1 building to Z2		10 minutes Z1				
2 x 3 minutes building over the 3 minutes from Z2 to Z4		10 minutes building to Z2				
4 minutes Z2 running		*Main set*				
15 minutes Z2 running		Aim to hold a Z1/Z2 effort – where possible target Z2				
Main set		Include walk breaks when necessary. A couple of minutes every 20-60 minutes is recommended.				
4 x 4 minutes						
Each 4-minute block is broken into 1/2/1: the first minute is Z1/2, the next two minutes are Z4 and the final minute is Z5b		*Cool down*				
		10 minutes easy Z1 running				
Cool down						
10 minutes easy Z1 running						
Walk & stretch as needed						

WEEK 4: 21 WEEKS TO RACE DAY – BASE PHASE 1 – RECOVERY WEEK

Monday	Tuesday	Wednesday	Thursday	Friday	Saturday	Sunday
Easy strides	**Recovery day**	**Long run – trail**	**Recovery techniques**	**Fitness test No 3 – uphill time trial**	**Soul run – trail**	Day off
Total time: 50 minutes	Schedule a remedial massage if possible	2 hours 50 minutes	20–30 minutes	Refer to Chapter 4	1 hour 40 minutes	
Warm-up		*Warm-up*	Refer to Chapter 12	*If an additional day of rest is required, shift this set to Saturday and remove the Saturday soul run. Instead, complete an easy 30-minute Z2 recovery run.*	Aim to gradually build into your running over the first 10 minutes	
10 minutes Z1		10 minutes Z1				
10 minutes Z2		10 minutes building to Z2				
Main set		*Main set*				
10 x 1-minute strides		Aim to hold a Z1/Z2 effort – where possible target Z2				
Complete 10 x 1 strides at Z3 on a 1-minute Z2 recovery.		Include walk breaks when necessary. A couple of minutes every 20-60 minutes is recommended.				
Try to run according to feel and keep the strides comfortable and easy		Include one 30-minute segment of Z3 running. Aim to complete this segment on a prolonged uphill if possible.				
Cool down		*Cool down*				
10 minutes easy Z1 running		10 minutes easy Z1 running				
Walk & stretch as needed						
If you feel more recovery is required change this set to a 30-minute Z2 recovery run						

PROGRAM THREE

WEEK 5: 20 WEEKS TO RACE DAY – BASE PHASE 2

Monday	Tuesday	Wednesday	Thursday	Friday	Saturday	Sunday
12 minute ramps	**Easy recovery run**	**Long run – trail**	**Day off**	**4/3/2/1 Max intensity builds**	**Soul run – trail**	Day off
Total time: 69 minutes	30 minutes Z2	3 hours	**Recovery techniques**	Total time: 60 minutes	1 hour 50 minutes	
Warm-up	Spend the first 10 minutes build-ing to Z2	*Warm-up*	20–30 minutes	*Warm-up*	Aim to gradually build into your running over the first 10 minutes	
10 minutes Z1 building to Z2		10 minutes Z1	Refer to Chapter 12	10 minutes Z1 building to Z2		
2 x 3 minutes building over the 3 minutes from Z2 to Z4		10 minutes building to Z2		4 x 1-minute strides on a 1-minute easy jogging recovery		
Main set		*Main set*		12 minutes Z2		
3 x 12 minute builds:		Aim to hold a Z1/Z2 effort – where possible target Z2		*Main set*		
3 minutes Z2		Include walk breaks when necessary. A couple of minutes every 20–60 minutes is recom-mended.		Take the first 30 seconds to build into each of the efforts.		
3 minutes Z3				4 minutes Z5b 4 minute Z2		
3 minutes Z4				3 minutes Z5b 3 minute Z2		
3 minutes Z5b				2 minutes Z5b 2 minute Z2		
At the conclusion of each block include a 1-minute walk.		*Cool down*		1 minute Z5b 1 minute Z2		
Cool down		10 minutes easy Z1 running		*Cool down*		
10 minutes easy Z1 running				10 minutes easy Z1 running		
Walk & stretch as needed				Walk & stretch as needed		

WEEK 6: 19 WEEKS TO RACE DAY – BASE PHASE 2

Monday	Tuesday	Wednesday	Thursday	Friday	Saturday	Sunday
Pyramid fartlek	**Easy recovery run**	**Long run – trail**	**Recovery techniques**	**Hard/easy**	**Soul run – trail**	**Day off**
Total time: 67 minutes	30 minutes Z2	3 hours 10 minutes	20–30 minutes	Total time: 60 minutes	2 hours	
Warm-up	Spend the first 10 minutes building to Z2	*Warm-up*	Refer to Chapter 12	*Warm-up*	Aim to gradually build into your running over the first 10 minutes	
10 minutes Z1 building to Z2		10 minutes Z1		10 minutes Z1 building to Z2		
2 x 3 minutes building over the 3 minutes from Z2 to Z4		10 minutes building to Z2		4 x 1-minute strides on a 1-minute easy jogging recovery		
Main set		*Main set*		2 minutes Z2		
Complete the following pyramid alternating between Z2 and Z4:		Aim to hold a Z1/Z2 effort – where possible target Z2		*Main set*		
4 minutes Z4		Include walk breaks when necessary. A couple of minutes every 20–60 minutes is recommended.		15 x 1 minutes on a 1-minute Z2 recovery:		
5 minutes Z2				1–8 at Z4		
6 minutes Z4		*Cool down*		9–15 at Z5a		
7 minutes Z2		10 minutes easy Z1 running		*Cool down*		
6 minutes Z4				10 minutes easy Z1 running		
5 minutes Z2				Walk & stretch as needed		
4 minutes Z4				Be aware that HR will not respond completely during the efforts so you will have to rely on your feel for your output or RPE		
Cool down						
10 minutes easy Z1 running						
Walk & stretch as needed						

WEEK 7: 18 WEEKS TO RACE DAY – BASE PHASE 2

Monday	Tuesday	Wednesday	Thursday	Friday	Saturday	Sunday
12-minute ramps	**Easy recovery run**	**Long run – trail**	**Recovery techniques**	**Pyramid down**	**Soul run – trail**	Day off
Total time: 82 minutes	30 minutes	3 hours 20 minutes	20–30 minutes	Total time: approx. 60 minutes	2 hours 10 minutes	
Warm-up	Spend the first 10 minutes building to Z2	*Warm-up*	Refer to Chapter 12	*Warm-up*	Aim to gradually build into your running over the first 10 minutes	
10 minutes Z1 building to Z2		10 minutes Z1		10 minutes Z1 building to Z2		
2 x 3 minutes building over the 3 minutes from Z2 to Z4		10 minutes building to Z2		4 x 1-minute strides on a 1-minute easy jogging recovery		
Main set		*Main set*		2 minutes Z2		
4 x 12 minute builds:		Aim to hold a Z1/Z2 effort – where possible target Z2		*Main set*		
3 minutes Z2		Include walk breaks when necessary. A couple of minutes every 20–60 minutes is recommended.		Run straight through:		
3 minutes Z3				6 minutes Z2 1 minute Z5b		
3 minutes Z4		Include one 20-minute segment of Zone 3 running. Aim to complete this segment on a prolonged uphill if possible.		5 minutes Z2 1 minute Z5b		
3 minutes Z5b				4 minutes Z2 1 minute Z5b		
At the conclusion of each block include a 1 minute walk.				3 minutes Z2 1 minute Z5b		
Cool down		*Cool down*		2 minutes Z2 1 minute Z5b		
10 minutes easy Z1 running		10 minutes easy Z1 running		1 minutes Z2 1 minute Z5b		
Walk & stretch as needed				*Cool down*		
				10 minutes easy Z1 running		
				Walk & stretch as needed		

WEEK 8: 17 WEEKS TO RACE DAY – BASE PHASE 2 – RECOVERY WEEK

Monday	Tuesday	Wednesday	Thursday	Friday	Saturday	Sunday
6 squared run	**Day off**	**Long run – trail**	**Recovery techniques**	**Hill reps 6 x 3 minutes**	**Soul run – trail**	Day off
Total time: 66 minutes	Schedule a remedial massage if possible	3 hours 30 minutes	20–30 minutes	Total time: approx. 75 minutes	2 hour 20 minutes	
Warm-up		Warm-up	Refer to Chapter 12	Warm-up	Aim to gradually build into your running over the first 10 minutes	
10 minutes Z1 building to Z2		10 minutes Z1		10 minutes Z1 building to Z2		
2 x 3 minutes building over the 3 minutes from Z2 to Z4		10 minutes building to Z2		4 x1-minute strides on a 1-minute easy jogging recovery		
Main set		Main set		2 minutes Z2		
6 x 6 minutes:		Aim to hold a Z1/Z2 effort – where possible target Z2		Main set		
3 minutes Z2				6 x 3-minute hill reps building to Z5b on an easy Z1 descent and 60 seconds RI		
2 minutes Z3		Include walk breaks when necessary. A couple of minutes every 20–60 minutes is recommended.		This means that you run the hill or part of a hill from a chosen start point for 3 minutes duration. At this point hit the lap button on your watch. Turn for an easy recovery jog down the hill.		
1 minute Z4		Include one 30-minute segment of Zone 3 running. Aim to complete this segment on a prolonged uphill if possible.		Upon reaching your start point have a 60-second rest and then repeat. Complete this for a total of six reps.		
Cool down		Cool down		Cool down		
10 minutes easy Z1 running		10 minutes easy Z1 running		10 minutes easy Z1 running		
Walk & stretch as needed				Walk & stretch as needed		
If you feel more recovery is required change this set to a 30-minute Z2 recovery run						

WEEK 9: 16 WEEKS TO RACE DAY – BASE PHASE 3

Monday	Tuesday	Wednesday	Thursday	Friday	Saturday	Sunday
Uphill effort – 15 minutes	**Easy recovery run**	**Long run – trail**	**Recovery techniques**	**Hill reps 7x 3 minutes**	**Soul run – trail**	Day off
Total time: 80 minutes	20 minutes Z2	3 hours 40 minutes	20–30 minutes	Total time: approx. 80 minutes	2 hours 30 minutes	
Warm-up	Spend the first 10 minutes build-ing to Z2	*Warm-up*	Refer to Chapter 12	*Warm-up*	Aim to gradually build into your running over the first 10 minutes	
10 minutes Z1 building to Z2		10 minutes Z1		10 minutes Z1 building to Z2		
2 x 3 minutes building over the 3 minutes from Z2 to Z4		10 minutes building to Z2		4 x 1-minute strides on a 1-minute easy jogging recovery		
10 minutes Z2		*Main set*		2 minutes Z2		
Main set		Aim to hold a Z1/Z2 effort – where possible target Z2		*Main set*		
1 x 15 minutes uphill effort Z4		Include walk breaks when necessary. A couple of minutes every 20–60 minutes is recommended.		7 x 3-minute hill reps building to Z5b on an easy Z1 descent and 60 seconds RI		
After completing the effort continue to the top of the hill or to an appropriate point that will allow an approx. 80 minute run. Following the effort continue at a Z2 intensity.		*Cool down*		As per last week, but this time adding another rep		
On the descent target a Z2 intensity where possible; however, be aware that you will likely also spend consider-able time in Z1 and this is fine		10 minutes easy Z1 running		*Cool down*		
Cool down				10 minutes easy Z1 running		
10 minutes easy Z1 running				Walk & stretch as needed		
Walk & stretch as needed						

WEEK 10: 15 WEEKS TO RACE DAY – BASE PHASE 3

Monday	Tuesday	Wednesday	Thursday	Friday	Saturday	Sunday
Uphill effort – 20 minutes	**Easy recovery run**	**Long run – trail**	**Recovery techniques**	**Hill reps 5 x 5 minutes**	**Soul run – trail**	Day off
Total time: 80 minutes	35 minutes Z2	3 hours 50 minutes	20–30 minutes	Total time: approx. 80 minutes	2 hours 40 minutes	
Warm-up	Spend the first 10 minutes building to Z2	*Warm-up*	Refer to Chapter 12	*Warm-up*	Aim to gradually build into your running over the first 10 minutes	
10 minutes Z1 building to Z2		10 minutes Z1		10 minutes Z1 building to Z2		
2 x 3 minutes building over the 3 minutes from Z2 to Z4		10 minutes building to Z2		4 x 1minute strides on a 1-minute easy jogging recovery		
10 minutes Z2		*Main set*		2 minutes Z2		
Main set		Aim to hold a Z1/Z2 effort – where possible target Z2		*Main set*		
1 x 20 minutes uphill effort Z4		Include walk breaks when necessary. A couple of minutes every 20–60 minutes is recommended.		5 x 5 minute hill reps building to Z5a on an easy Z1 descent and 60 seconds RI		
After completing the effort continue to the top of the hill or to an appropriate point that will allow an approx. 80 minute run. Following the effort continue at a Z2 intensity.		*Cool down*		*Cool down*		
On the descent target a Z2 intensity where possible; however, be aware that you will likely also spend consider-able time in Z1 and this is fine		10 minutes easy Z1 running		10 minutes easy Z1 running		
Cool down				Walk & stretch as needed		
10 minutes easy Z1 running						
Walk & stretch as needed						

WEEK 11: 14 WEEKS TO RACE DAY – BASE PHASE 3

Monday	Tuesday	Wednesday	Thursday	Friday	Saturday	Sunday
Uphill effort – 3 x 10 minutes	**Easy recovery run**	**Long run – trail**	**Recovery techniques**	**Hill reps 6 x 5 minutes**	**Soul run – trail**	**Day off**
Total time: 80–90 minutes	30 minutes Z2	4 hours	20–30 minutes	Total time: approx. 80 minutes	2 hours 50 minutes	
Warm-up	Spend the first 10 minutes building to Z2	*Warm-up*	Refer to Chapter 12	*Warm-up*	Aim to gradually build into your running over the first 10 minutes	
10 minutes Z1 building to Z2		10 minutes Z1		10 minutes Z1 building to Z2		
2 x 3 minutes building over the 3 minutes from Z2 to Z4		10 minutes building to Z2		4 x 1-minute strides on a 1-minute easy jogging recovery		
Main set		*Main set*		2 minutes Z2		
3 x 10 minutes uphill effort:		Aim to hold a Z1/Z2 effort – where possible target Z2		*Main set*		
1 x 10 minutes Z3		Include walk breaks when necessary. A couple of minutes every 20–60 minutes is recommended.		6 x 5-minute hill reps Z4 on an easy Z1 descent		
2 x 10 minutes Z4				*Cool down*		
All on a 4-minute Z2 recovery		*Cool down*		10 minutes easy Z1 running		
After completing the effort continue to the top of the hill or to an appropriate point that will allow an approx. 80 minute run. Following the effort continue at a Z2 intensity.		10 minutes easy Z1 running		Walk & stretch as needed		
On the descent target a Z2 intensity where possible, however, be aware that you will likely also spend considerable time in Z1 and this is fine						
Cool down						
10 minutes easy Z1 running						
Walk & stretch as needed						

Monday	Tuesday	Wednesday	Thursday	Friday	Saturday	Sunday
Easy recovery run	**Day off**	**Long run – trail**	**Recovery techniques**	**4/3/2/1 max intensity builds**	**Soul run – trail**	**Day off**
Total time: 60 minutes	Schedule a remedial massage if possible	4 hours 15 minutes	20–30 minutes	Total time: 60 minutes	3 hours	
Warm-up:		Warm-up	Refer to Chapter 12	Warm-up	Aim to gradually build into your running over the first 10 minutes	
10 minutes Z1		10 minutes Z1		10 minutes Z1 building to Z2		
10 minutes building to Z2		10 minutes building to Z2		4 x 1-minute strides on a 1-minute easy jogging recovery		
Easy 30-minute Z2 run		Main set		2 minutes Z2		
This can be completed on the trails or road.		Aim to hold a Z1/Z2 effort – where possible target Z2		Main set		
Cool down		Include walk breaks when necessary. A couple of minutes every 20-60 minutes is recommended.		Take the first 30 seconds to build into each of the efforts.		
10 minutes easy Z1		Include one 30-minute segment of Zone 3 running. Aim to complete this segment on a prolonged uphill if possible.		4 minutes Z5b 4 minute Z2		
		Cool down		3 minutes Z5b 3 minute Z2		
		10 minutes easy Z1 running		2 minutes Z5b 2 minute Z2		
				1 minute Z5b 1 minute Z2		
				Cool down		
				10 minutes easy Z1 running		
				Walk & stretch as needed		

291

WEEK 13: 12 WEEKS TO RACE DAY – BUILD PHASE 1

Monday	Tuesday	Wednesday	Thursday	Friday	Saturday	Sunday
Uphill effort – 3 x 10 minutes	**Easy recovery run**	**Long run – trail**	**Recovery techniques**	**Hill reps 6 x 5 minutes**	**Soul run – trail**	Day off
Total time: 80–90 minutes	30 minutes Z2	4 hours 30 minutes	20–30 minutes	Total time: approx. 80 minutes	2 hours 50 minutes	
Warm-up	Spend the first 10 minutes building to Z2.	*Warm-up*	Refer to Chapter 12	*Warm-up*	Aim to gradually build into your running over the first 10 minutes	
10 minutes Z1 building to Z2		10 minutes Z1		10 minutes Z1 building to Z2		
2 x 3 minutes building over the 3 minutes from Z2 to Z4		10 minutes building to Z2		4 x 1-minute strides on a 1-minute easy jogging recovery		
Main set		*Main set*		2 minutes Z2		
3 x 10 minutes uphill effort:		Aim to hold a Z1/Z2 effort – where possible target Z2		*Main set*		
1 x 10 minutes Z3				6 x 5=minute hill reps Z4 on a 4-minute easy Z1 descent		
2 x 10 minutes Z4		Include walk breaks when necessary. A couple of minutes every 20–60 minutes is recommended.		This means that you will not quite return to your start point during this time and so will gradually make it further and further up the hill		
All on a 4-minute Z2 recovery						
After completing the effort continue to the top of the hill or to an appropriate point that will allow an approx. 80-minute run. Following the effort continue at a Z2 intensity.		*Cool down*				
		10 minutes easy Z1 running		*Cool down*		
On the descent target a Z2 intensity where possible; however, be aware that you will likely also spend considerable time in Z1 and this is fine				10 minutes easy Z1 running		
Cool down				Walk & stretch as needed		
10 minutes easy Z1 running						
Walk & stretch as needed						

Monday	Tuesday	Wednesday	Thursday	Friday	Saturday	Sunday
Uphill effort – 15/10/5 minutes	**Easy recovery run**	**Long run – trail**	**Recovery techniques**	**Hill reps 3 x 8/4 minutes**	**Soul run – trail**	Day off
Total time: 80–90 minutes	35 minutes	4 hours 45 minutes	20–30 minutes	Total time: approx. 80 minutes	2 hours 50 minutes	
Warm-up	Z2	*Warm-up*	Refer to Chapter 12	*Warm-up*	Aim to gradually build into your running over the first 10 minutes	
10 minutes Z1 building to Z2	Spend the first 10 minutes building to Z2	10 minutes Z1		10 minutes Z1 building to Z2		
2 x 3 minutes building over the 3 minutes from Z2 to Z4		10 minutes building to Z2		4 x 1-minute strides on a 1-minute easy jogging recovery		
Main set		*Main set*		2 minutes Z2		
1 x 15 minutes Z3		Aim to hold a Z1/Z2 effort – where possible target Z2		*Main set*		
1 x 10 minutes Z4		Include walk breaks when necessary.		3 x 12 minutes as 8 minutes Z3 into 4 minutes Z4 on a 4-minute easy Z1 descent. Turn and repeat.		
1 x 5 minutes Z4		A couple of minutes every 20–60 minutes is recommended.		This means that you will not quite return to your start point during this time and so will gradually make it further and further up the hill		
All on a 4-minute Z2 recovery		*Cool down*		*Cool down*		
After completing the effort continue to the top of the hill or to an appropriate point that will allow an approx. 80-minute run. Following the effort continue at a Z2 intensity.		10 minutes easy Z1 running		10 minutes easy Z1 running		
On the descent target a Z2 intensity where possible; however, be aware that you will likely also spend considerable time in Z1 and this is fine				Walk & stretch as needed		
Cool down						
10 minutes easy Z1 running						
Walk & stretch as needed						

WEEK 15: 10 WEEKS TO RACE DAY – BUILD PHASE 1

Monday	Tuesday	Wednesday	Thursday	Friday	Saturday	Sunday
Uphill effort – 15/10/5 minutes	**Easy recovery run**	**Long run – trail**	**Recovery techniques**	**Hill Reps 3 x 8/4 minutes**	**Soul run – trail**	Day off
Total time: 80–90 minutes	40 minutes Z2	5 hours	20–30 minutes	Total time: approx. 80 minutes	3 hours	
Warm-up	Spend the first 10 minutes building to Z2	*Warm-up*	Refer to Chapter 12	*Warm-up*	Aim to gradually build into your running over the first 10 minutes	
10 minutes Z1 building to Z2		10 minutes Z1		10 minutes Z1 building to Z2		
2 x3 minutes building over the 3 minutes from Z2 to Z4		10 minutes building to Z2		4 x 1-minute strides on a 1-minute easy jogging recovery		
Main set		*Main set*		2 minutes Z2		
15/10/5 minutes uphill effort as follows:		Aim to hold a Z1/Z2 effort – where possible target Z2		*Main set*		
15 minutes Z4 on a 6-minute Z2 recovery				3 x 12 minutes as 8 minutes Z3 into 4 minutes Z4 on a 4-minute easy Z1 descent. Turn and repeat.		
10 minutes Z4 on a 4-minute Z2 recovery		Include walk breaks when necessary. A couple of minutes every 20–60 minutes is recommended.		This means that you will not quite return to your start point during this time and so will gradually make it further and further up the hill		
5 minutes Z4 followed by a 2-minute walk for a job well done				*Cool down*		
After completing the effort continue to the top of the hill or to an appropriate point that will allow an approx. 80-minute run. Following the effort continue at a Z2 intensity		*Cool down*		10 minutes easy Z1 running		
On the descent target a Z2 intensity where possible; however, be aware that you will likely also spend considerable time in Z1 and this is fine		10 minutes easy Z1 running		Walk & stretch as needed		
Hint: it is recommended that you start at the lower end of Z4 for the first 15-minute block. You can then increase the intensity towards the upper end of Z4 over the 10 and 5-minute period if needed.						
Cool down						
10 minutes easy Z1 running						
Walk & stretch as needed						

294

Monday	Tuesday	Wednesday	Thursday	Friday	Saturday	Sunday
Easy strides	Day off	Long run – trail	Recovery techniques	Hill reps 6 x 6 minutes	Soul run – trail	Day off
Total time: 50 minutes	Schedule a remedial massage if possible	5 hours 15 minutes	20–30 minutes	Total time: approx. 80 minutes	3 hours	
Warm-up		Warm-up	Refer to Chapter 12	Warm-up	Aim to gradually build into your running over the first 10 minutes	
10 minutes Z1		10 minutes Z1		10 minutes Z1 building to Z2		
10 minutes Z2		10 minutes building to Z2		4 x 1-minute strides on a 1-minute easy jogging recovery		
Main set		Main set		2 minutes Z2		
10 x 1-minute strides		Aim to hold a Z1/Z2 effort – where possible target Z2		Main set		
Complete 10 x1-minute strides Z3 on a 1-minute Z2 recovery.		Include walk breaks when necessary. A couple of minutes every 20–60 minutes is recommended.		6 x 6 minute hill reps:		
Try to run on feel and keep the strides comfortable and easy.		Cool down		1 & 2 at Z3		
Cool down		10 minutes easy Z1 running		3–6 at Z4		
10 minutes easy Z1 running				All on a 4-minute easy Z1 descent		
Walk & stretch as needed				This means that you will not quite return to your start point during this time and so will gradually make it further and further up the hill		
*If you're feeling more recovery is required, change this set to a 30-minute Z2 recovery run.				Cool down		
				10 minutes easy Z1 running		
				Walk & stretch as needed		

295

WEEK 17: 8 WEEKS TO RACE DAY – BUILD PHASE 2

Monday	Tuesday	Wednesday	Thursday	Friday	Saturday	Sunday
Split the hill	**Easy recovery run**	**Long run – trail**	**Recovery techniques**	**Hill reps 7 x 6 minutes**	**Soul run – trail**	Day off
Total time: 80–90 minutes	40 minutes Z2	5 hours 30 minutes	20–30 minutes	Total time: approx. 90 minutes	3 hours	
Warm-up	Spend the first 10 minutes building to Z2.	*Warm-up*	Refer to Chapter 12	*Warm-up*	Aim to gradually build into your running over the first 10 minutes	
10 minutes Z1 building to Z2		10 minutes Z1 10 minutes building to Z2		10 minutes Z1 building to Z2		
2 x 3 minutes building over the 3 minutes from Z2 to Z4				4 x 1-minute strides on a 1-minute easy jogging recovery		
Main set		*Main set*				
2 x 15-minute uphill efforts		Aim to hold a Z1/Z2 effort – where possible target Z2		2 minutes Z2		
1 x 15-minute Z4 on a 6-minute Z2 recovery				*Main set*		
1 x 15-minute Z4		Include walk breaks when necessary. A couple of minutes every 20–60 minutes is recommended.		7 x 6 minute hill reps:		
After completing the effort continue to the top of the hill or to an appropriate point that will allow an approx. 80-minute run. Following the effort continue at a Z2 intensity.				1 & 2 at Z3		
				3–7 at Z4		
		Cool down		All on a 4-minute easy Z1 descent		
On the descent target a Z2 intensity where possible; however, be aware that you will likely also spend considerable time in Z1 and this is fine		10 minutes easy Z1 running		This means that you will not quite return to your start point during this time and so will gradually make it further and further up the hill		
Hint: it is recommended that you start at the lower end of Z4 for the first 15-minute block. You can then increase the intensity towards the upper end of Z4 over the 10 and 5-minute period if needed.				*Cool down*		
Cool down				10 minutes easy Z1 running		
10 minutes easy Z1 running				Walk & stretch as needed		
Walk & stretch as needed						

Monday	Tuesday	Wednesday	Thursday	Friday	Saturday	Sunday
Split the hill 2 x 15 minutes	**Easy recovery run**	**Long run – trail**	**Recovery techniques**	**Hill reps 7 x 6 minutes**	**Soul run – trail**	**Day off**
Total time: 80 minutes	40 minutes Z2	4 hours	20–30 minutes	Total time: approx. 90 minutes	4 hours	
Warm-up	Spend the first 10 minutes building to Z2	*Warm-up*	Refer to Chapter 12	*Warm-up*	Aim to gradually build into your running over the first 10 minutes	
10 minutes Z1 building to Z2		10 minutes Z1		10 minutes Z1 building to Z2		
2 x 3 minutes building over the 3 minutes from Z2 to Z4		10 minutes building to Z2		4 x 1-minute strides on a 1-minute easy jogging recovery		
Main set		*Main set*		2 minutes Z2		
2 x 15 minute uphill efforts as follows:		Aim to hold a Z1/Z2 effort – where possible target Z2		*Main set*		
15 minutes Z4 on a 5-minute Z2 recovery		Include walk breaks when necessary.		7 x 6 minute hill reps:		
15 minutes Z4		A couple of minutes every 20–60 minutes is recommended.		1 & 2 at Z3		
After completing the effort continue to the top of the hill or to an appropriate point that will allow an approx. 80 minute run. Following the effort continue at a Z2 intensity.		*Cool down*		3–7 at Z4		
On the descent target a Z2 intensity where possible; however, be aware that you will likely also spend considerable time in Z1 and this is fine		10 minutes easy Z1 running		All on a 4-minute easy Z1 descent		
Hint: as per the 15/10/5 run, it is recommended that you start at the lower end of Z4 for the first 15-minute block. You can then increase the intensity towards the upper end of Z4 over the subsequent 15-minute block if needed. But do not aim to go above Z4.				This means that you will not quite return to your start point during this time and so will gradually make it further and further up the hill		
Cool down				*Cool down*		
10 minutes easy Z1 running				10 minutes easy Z1 running		
Walk & stretch as needed				Walk & stretch as needed		

WEEK 19: 6 WEEKS TO RACE DAY – BUILD PHASE 2

Monday	Tuesday	Wednesday	Thursday	Friday	Saturday	Sunday
Full hill 1 x 30 minutes	**Easy recovery run**	**Race simulation day**	**Recovery techniques**	**Soul run – trail**	**Hill reps 7 x 6 minutes**	Day off
Total time: 80–90 minutes	40 minutes Z2	**Long run**	20–30 minutes	90 minutes	Total time: approx. 100 minutes	
Warm-up	Spend the first 10 minutes building to Z2	6 hours	Refer to Chapter 12	Aim to gradually build into your running over the first 10 minutes	*Warm-up*	
10 minutes Z1 building to Z2		*Warm-up*			10 minutes Z1 building to Z2	
2 x 3 minutes building over the 3 minutes from Z2 to Z4		10 minutes Z1			4 x 1-minute strides on a 1-minute easy jogging recovery	
Main set		10 minutes building to Z2			2 minutes Z2	
1 x 30-minute Z4 uphill effort		*Main set*			*Main set*	
After completing the effort continue to the top of the hill or to an appropriate point that will allow an approx. 80-minute run. Following the effort continue at a Z2 intensity.		Aim to hold a Z1/Z2 effort – where possible target Z2			7 x 6 minute hill reps:	
On the descent target a Z2 intensity where possible; however, be aware that you will likely also spend considerable time in Z1 and this is fine		Include walk breaks when necessary. A couple of minutes every 20–60 minutes is recommended.			1 & 2 at Z3
3–7 at Z4
All on a 4-minute easy Z1 descent	
Hint: as per the 15/10/5 run, it is recommended that you start at the lower end of Z4 for the first 15-minute block. You can then increase the intensity towards the upper end of Z4 over the subsequent 15-minute block if needed. But do not aim to go above Z4.		*Cool down*			This means that you will not quite return to your start point during this time and so will gradually make it further and further up the hill	
Cool down		10 minutes easy Z1 running			*Cool down*	
10 minutes easy Z1 running					10 minutes easy Z1 running	
Walk & stretch as needed					Walk & stretch as needed	

WEEK 20: 5 WEEKS TO RACE DAY – BUILD PHASE 2 (RECOVERY WEEK)

Monday	Tuesday	Wednesday	Thursday	Friday	Saturday	Sunday
Easy strides	**Day off**	**Long run**	**Recovery techniques**	**Hill reps 7 x 6 minutes**	**Soul run – trail**	Day off
Total time: 50 minutes	Schedule a remedial massage if possible	4.5 hours	20–30 minutes	Total time: approx. 100 minutes	2 hours	
Warm-up		Warm-up	Refer to Chapter 12	Warm-up	Aim to gradually build into your running over the first 10 minutes	
10 minutes Z1		10 minutes Z1		10 minutes Z1 building to Z2		
10 minutes Z2		10 minutes building to Z2		4 x 1-minute strides on a 1 minute easy jogging recovery		
Main set		Main set		2 minutes Z2		
10 x 1 minute strides		Aim to hold a Z1/Z2 effort – where possible target Z2		Main set		
Complete 10 x 1-minute strides at Z3 on a 1-minute Z2 recovery.		Include walk breaks when necessary. A couple of minutes every 20–60 minutes is recommended.		7 x 6 minute hill reps:		
Try to run to feel and keep the strides comfortable and easy.				1 & 2 at Z3		
		Cool down		3–7 at Z4		
Cool down		10 easy Z1 running		All on a 4-minute easy Z1 descent		
10 minutes easy Z1 running				This means that you will not quite return to your start point during this time and so will gradually make it further and further up the hill		
Walk & stretch as needed				Cool down		
*If you are feeling more recovery is required, change this set to a 30-minute Z2 recovery run.				10 minutes easy Z1 running		
				Walk & stretch as needed		

WEEK 21: 4 WEEKS TO RACE DAY (PEAK WEEK)

Monday	Tuesday	Wednesday	Thursday	Friday	Saturday	Sunday
Fitness test No 2 – 60 minute aerobic threshold test Total time: 90 minutes Refer to Chapter 4	Day off	**Race simulation** 5 hours *Warm-up* 10 minutes Z1 10 minutes building to Z2 *Main set* Aim to hold a Z1/Z2 effort – where possible target Z2 Include walk breaks when necessary. A couple of minutes every 20-60 minutes is recommended. *Cool down* 10 minutes easy Z1 running	**Recovery techniques** 20–30 minutes Refer to Chapter 12	**Soul run – trail** 40 minutes Aim to gradually build into your running over the first 10 minutes	**Race simulation** 5 hours *Warm-up* 10 minutes Z1 10 minutes building to Z2 *Main set* Aim to hold a Z1/Z2 effort – where possible target Z2 Include walk breaks when necessary. A couple of minutes every 20–60 minutes is recommended. *Cool down* 10 minutes easy Z1 running	Day off

Monday	Tuesday	Wednesday	Thursday	Friday	Saturday	Sunday
Walk	**Easy recovery run**	**Soul run – trail**	**Recovery techniques**	**Hill reps 3 x 6/4 minutes**	**Long run (short)**	Day off
20-30 minutes	20 minutes Z2	80 minutes	20-30 minutes	Total time: Approx. 80 minutes	90 minutes	
Stretch as needed	Spend the first 10 minutes building to Z2.	Aim to gradually build into your running over the first 10 minutes	Refer to Chapter 12	*Warm-up*	*Warm-up*	
				10 minutes Z1 building to Z2	10 minutes Z1	
		If needed this can also be changed to an easy recovery run		4 x 1-minute strides on a 1-minute easy jogging recovery	10 minutes building to Z2	
				2 minutes Z2	*Main set*	
				Main set	Aim to hold a Z1/Z2 effort – where possible target Z2	
				3 x 12 minutes: 6 minutes Z3 into 4 minutes Z4 on a 4-minute easy Z1 descent. Turn and repeat.	Include walk breaks when necessary. A couple of minutes every 20–60 minutes is recommended.	
				This means that you will not quite return to your start point during this time and so will gradually make it further and further up the hill	Include one 30-minute segment of Z3 running. Aim to complete this segment on a prolonged uphill section if possible.	
				Cool down	*Cool down*	
				10 minutes easy Z1 running	10 Easy Z1 running	
				Walk & stretch as needed		
				Visualisation session		

PROGRAM THREE

PROGRAM THREE

WEEK 23: 2 WEEKS TO RACE DAY – TAPER 2

Monday	Tuesday	Wednesday	Thursday	Friday	Saturday	Sunday
Fitness test No 3 Refer to Chapter 4 Alternatively, last intensity session as below **Hill reps 3 x 8/4 minutes** Total time: Approx. 80 minutes *Warm-up* 10 minutes Z1 building to Z2 4 x1-minute strides on a 1-minute easy jogging recovery 2 minutes Z2 *Main set* 3 x 12 minutes: 8 minutes Z3 into 4 minutes Z4 on a 4-minute easy Z1 descent. Turn and repeat. This means that you will not quite return to your start point during this time and so will gradually make it further and further up the hill *Cool down* 10 minutes easy Z1 running Walk & stretch as needed **Visualisation session**	**Day off** Walk as needed	**Long run (short)** 90 minutes *Warm-up* 10 minutes Z1 10 minutes building to Z2 *Main set* Aim to hold a Z1/Z2 effort – where possible target Z2 Include walk breaks when necessary. A couple of minutes every 20–60 minutes is recommended. Include one 30-minute segment of Z3 running. Aim to complete this segment on a prolonged uphill section if possible. *Cool down* 10 minutes easy Z1 running	**Recovery techniques** 20–30 minutes Refer to Chapter 12	**Easy recovery run** 30 minutes Z2 Try to spend the first 10 minutes building to Z2. **Visualisation session**	**Soul run – trail** 1 hour Aim to gradually build into your running over the first 10 minutes	**Day off**

302

WEEK 24: 1 WEEK TO RACE DAY BUILD – TAPER 1 (RACE WEEK)

Monday	Tuesday	Wednesday	Thursday	Friday	Saturday	Sunday
Easy recovery run 30 minutes Easy Z1/ Z2 run & stretching Massage if needed (recommended) but the massage must occur after the run.	Travel followed by a short 20-minute walk	**Easy run** 40 minutes with short intensity segments *Warm-up* 10 minutes Z1 building to Z2 4 x 1-minute strides on a 1-minute easy jogging recovery 2 minutes Z2 *Main set* 4 x 2 minutes Z3 on a 1-minute Z2 recovery *Cool down* 5-10 minutes easy Z1 **Visualisation Session**	**Easy recovery run** 20 minutes Z1/Z2 **Stretching** Carbohydrate-rich meal for dinner	**Day off** If you can cope, or a very easy 20-minute run Event check-in and race briefing CHO loading **Optional** visualisation session	**Race day – the ultra graduation** You have done the work, trust yourself, believe in yourself and your ability. You will do great. **Time to smash your 100km ultramara-thon**	**Party time & recovery time**

ACKNOWLEDGEMENTS

To all the great coaches, teachers and mentors I have had in all my endeavours. You have all taught me, inspired me and helped shape my views, allowing me to become the coach and educator that I am, and allowing me to achieve my impossible.

While there are too many to mention here, I would especially like to thank:

Bob Carter

Deb McMahon

Grant Giles

Joe Friel

Kevin Fergusson

Nigel Pietsch

Wendy Piltz

The Burnside Lacrosse Club

The Lakers Triathlon Club

The exceptional teachers at East Adelaide Primary School

The equally exceptional teachers at Concordia College

All the athletes I have ever been fortunate enough to coach and assist on their personal journeys.

To Mum, Dad and Benjamin: let's just go with 'Thank you'.

A FINAL WORD

With your increased knowledge, you now have three options.

1. Follow this book and self-coach.

2. Find an ultra running coach to help you.

3. Disregard your new-found knowledge and do nothing!

But honestly, is that last point really an option? I want you to consider the investment that you're making in your ultra running, whether it's for one race or a series of races. What are you *really* putting into it? Time? Money? Effort? Emotion? Chances are you're investing all of these things in spades! It always amazes me how, despite making such a big investment, some people choose not to make a conscious effort to improve their trail and ultra running. But naturally I would say that; I'm a coach and one of the converted. ☺

Earlier in the book I planted a seed. A seed about how an ultra coach can fast-track your improvement and provide an approach tailored to you as an individual. Self-coaching or hiring a coach helps you to improve your ultra running and ultra running knowledge. This helps to ensure that you get the best return on your investment (time, money, effort, emotion) based on your personal circumstances. The great thing about coaching is that it gives you structure and accountability, and when you have that, you don't have to think – you just need to do.

Warning: coaching and training plug coming up. (Hey, it's what I love.)

If you're looking for an ultra running coach, this is where The Ultra Journey steps in. As the founder of The Ultra Journey, I believe everyone should be able to have fun training on the trails and running ultras. The Ultra Journey's mission is to deliver inspirational and educational ultra runner training programs leading to ultra runner improvement, accomplishment and celebration.

To help deliver this my team and I created The Ultra Journey coaching system. It is a training program matched with relevant videos to take you from wherever you are now to being a better ultra runner – one who achieves their impossible ultra running dreams.

The system takes you through the process outlined in this book of building up to your race. Over the years I have coached other runners and trained and raced myself, the process (or journey, if you like) that people progress through has become clear. While everyone's journey is different and unique, there are similarities, such as consistent questions and concerns that come up at predictable times. I have taken all this knowledge and jam-packed it into two programs: The Ultra Adventure and The Ultra Summit.

The Ultra Adventure is the twelve-week program that covers the basics of training leading into your goal ultra. This program starts on the Monday twelve weeks out from your goal race, and helps increase your knowledge of ultra running and training while preparing you for the race. This program has a focus of putting the basics in place and ensuring you're capable of making the distance of your goal ultra. It is suitable for ultras and trail races from 30–60km in length. (Yep, 30km is less than an ultra, but we understand that not everyone is going to jump straight into an ultramarathon, even though they aspire to complete one.) Whether your race is a 30km technical treat or a 60km elevation epic, we employ the same training principles while catering for your shorter distance. This helps build you up for your future goal.

The Ultra Summit is my pinnacle 24-week program. Starting the Monday twenty-four weeks out from your goal race, this program entails a full periodised training program, takes you through more advanced training methods and knowledge, and takes you step by step through how to utilise Training Peaks[23] to help track your ultra training.

Both options are paired with a structured training program that is appropriate for you and your personal goal race.

Your journey through the program will culminate with your ultra graduation, your impossible ultra race, which (all going well) you will finish in a blaze of glory. This is where you will show off to your friends and family all the personal improvement that you have been working towards, and all that you have learnt on your journey. You will have developed your ultra running and training knowledge – knowledge that will stay with you forever as you continue on your journey, reassess your goals and dream a bigger dream.

Some athletes will choose to self-coach, and there is absolutely no problem with this. If you choose this option, my hope is that the information in this book will help you to improve your ultra running. I hope that you will be able to implement this new knowl-

---

23   Training Peaks is the premier endurance coaching software

edge, along with your existing trail and ultra running knowledge, to follow a training plan that helps you reach your goals. From here I would encourage you to continue to find, implement and improve your ultra running knowledge as you continue on your great ultra running journey.

And if you do choose to coach yourself, The Ultra Journey's structured programs can still be a great option. Why? Because the knowledge you acquire through these programs will remain with you after you have finished the program and completed your goal race. On returning to self-coaching, you will understand and be able to implement the long-distance training principles covered in your preparation for your next ultra event. But of course, this is entirely up to you. Just saying! ☺

More information on the programs can be found on the Ultra Journey website: www.theultrajourney.com

I hope reading this book has convinced you that my advice is worth listening to. But if you're still not convinced, listen to what some of the athletes I have worked with are saying.

> *I came to Nick to have some accountability and assistance in reaching my ultra running goals. Juggling work, further study and three kids meant that I wanted to make sure I used the limited time I had effectively. The plan and guidance that Nick details allows me to achieve all this. As a result I have continued to improve and look forward to being at the start line of my next race. I don't know how I would have got to this point without your guidance, so thank you.*

AMANDA – ATHLETE, LAWYER, MOTHER, AVID TRAIL RUNNER

> *Thank you so much for all your support and encouragement. Thank you for training me, believing in me and assisting me in getting to the finish line of my first 100km ultramarathon.*

KAZU – WHO PLACED A MAGNIFICENT SECOND IN HER FIRST ULTRAMARATHON AND WENT ON TO WIN THE EVENT TWO YEARS LATER.

> *I couldn't have made it to the finish line without your help.*

ALAN – WHO FINISHED HIS FIRST 100KM ULTRAMARATHON ON A 36°C DAY, IN A RACE WITH A DNF RATE OF OVER 35% FOR THE GUYS AND 53% FOR THE GIRLS!

THANK YOU

As a little thank you for reading *Journey to 100*, a tree has been planted on your behalf. I believe in giving back, as does the whole team at The Ultra Journey, and we have decided to do it with trees. After all, as ultra runners we're fond of the environment, and we suspect you are too. This way we will always have somewhere special to run, for you, for ourselves and for our children.

Lightning Source UK Ltd.
Milton Keynes UK
UKHW02f0832041217
313844UK00009B/427/P